Contents

D0127934

Field Guides to Finding a New Career

Film and
Television

The Field Guides to Finding a New Career series

Field Guides to Finding a New Career

Film and Television

By S. J. Stratford

Checkmark Books®
An imprint of Infobase Publishing

Field Guides to Finding a New Career: Film and Television

Copyright © 2009 by Print Matters, Inc.

Checkmark Books
An imprint of Infobase Publishing
132 West 31st Street
New York, NY 10001

Library of Congress Cataloging-in-Publication Data

Stratford, S. J.
    Film and television / by S.J. Stratford.
        p. cm.—(Field guides to finding a new career)
    Includes bibliographical references and index.
    ISBN-13: 978-0-8160-7598-0 (alk. paper)
    ISBN-10: 0-8160-7598-0 (alk. paper)
    ISBN-13: 978-0-8160-7622-2 (alk. paper)
    ISBN-10: 0-8160-7622-7 (alk. paper)
1. Motion pictures—Vocational guidance.
2. Television—Vocational guidance. I. Title.
    PN1995.9.P75F54 2009
    791.4023—dc22

                                                    2008032007

Produced by Print Matters, Inc.
Text design by A Good Thing, Inc.
Illustrations by Molly Crabapple
Cover design by Takeshi Takahashi

Printed in the United States of America

Bang PMI 10 9 8 7 6 5 4 3 2 1

This book is printed on acid-free paper.

Introduction: Finding a New Career

Today, changing jobs is an accepted and normal part of life. In fact, according to the Bureau of Labor Statistics, Americans born between 1957 and 1964 held an average of 9.6 jobs from the ages of 18 to 36. The reasons for this are varied: To begin with, people live longer and healthier lives than they did in the past and accordingly have more years of active work life. However, the economy of the twenty-first century is in a state of constant and rapid change, and the workforce of the past does not always meet the needs of the future. Furthermore, fewer and fewer industries provide bonuses such as pensions and retirement health plans, which provide an incentive for staying with the same firm. Other workers experience epiphanies, spiritual growth, or various sorts of personal challenges that lead them to question the paths they have chosen.

Job instability is another prominent factor in the modern workplace. In the last five years, the United States has lost 2.6 *million jobs*; in 2005 alone, 370,000 workers were affected by mass layoffs. Moreover, because of new technology, changing labor markets, ageism, and a host of other factors, many educated, experienced professionals and skilled blue-collar workers have difficulty finding jobs in their former career tracks. Finally—and not just for women—the realities of juggling work and family life, coupled with economic necessity, often force radical revisions of career plans.

No matter how normal or accepted changing careers might be, however, the time of transition can also be a time of anxiety. Faced with the necessity of changing direction in the middle of their journey through life, many find themselves lost. Many career-changers find themselves asking questions such as: Where do I want to go from here? How do I get there? How do I prepare myself for the journey? Thankfully, the Field Guides to Finding a New Career are here to show the way. Using the language and visual style of a travel guide, we show you that reorienting yourself and reapplying your skills and knowledge to a new career is not an uphill slog, but an exciting journey of exploration. No matter whether you are in your twenties or close to retirement age, you can bravely set out to explore new paths and discover new vistas.

Though this series forms an organic whole, each volume is also designed to be a comprehensive, stand-alone, all-in-one guide to getting motivated, getting back on your feet, and getting back to work. We thoroughly discuss common issues such as going back to school, managing your household finances, putting your old skills to work in new situations, and selling yourself to potential employers. Each volume focuses on a broad career field, roughly grouped by Bureau of Labor Statistics' career clusters. Each chapter will focus on a particular career, suggesting new career paths suitable for an individual with that experience and training as well as practical issues involved in seeking and applying for a position.

Many times, the first question career-changers ask is, "Is this new path right for me?" Our self-assessment quiz, coupled with the career compasses at the beginning of each chapter, will help you to match your personal attributes to set you on the right track. Do you possess a storehouse of skilled knowledge? Are you the sort of person who puts others before yourself? Are you methodical and organized? Do you communicate effectively and clearly? Are you good at math? And how do you react to stress? All of these qualities contribute to career success—but they are not equally important in all jobs.

Many career-changers find working for themselves to be more hassle-free and rewarding than working for someone else. However, going at it alone, whether as a self-employed individual or a small-business owner, provides its own special set of challenges. Appendix A, "Going Solo: Starting Your Own Business," is designed to provide answers to many common questions and solutions to everyday problems, from income taxes to accounting to providing health insurance for yourself and your family.

For those who choose to work for someone else, how do you find a job, particularly when you have been out of the labor market for a while? Appendix B, "Outfitting Yourself for Career Success," is designed to answer these questions. It provides not only advice on résumé and self-presentation, but also the latest developments in looking for jobs, such as online resources, headhunters, and placement agencies. Additionally, it recommends how to explain an absence from the workforce to a potential employer.

Changing careers can be stressful, but it can also be a time of exciting personal growth and discovery. We hope that the Field Guides to Finding a New Career not only help you get your bearings in today's employment jungle but set you on the path to personal fulfillment, happiness, and prosperity.

How to Use this Book

Career Compasses

Each chapter begins with a series of "career compasses" to help you get your bearings and determine if this job is right for you, based on your answers to the self-assessment quiz at the beginning of the book. Does it require a mathematical mindset? Communication skills? Organizational skills? If you're not a "people person," a job requiring you to interact with the public might not be right for you. On the other hand, your organizational skills might be just what are needed in the back office.

Destination

A brief overview, giving you an introduction to the career, briefly explaining what it is, its advantages, why it is so satisfying, its growth potential, and its income potential.

You Are Here

A self-assessment asking you to locate yourself on your journey. Are you working in a related field? Are you working in a field where some skills will transfer? Or are you doing something completely different? In each case, we suggest ways to reapply your skills, gain new ones, and launch yourself on your new career path.

Navigating the Terrain

To help you on your way, we have provided a handy map showing the stages in your journey to a new career. "Navigating the Terrain" will show you the road you need to follow to get where you are going. Since the answers are not the same for everyone and every career, we are sure to show how there are multiple ways to get to the same destination.

Organizing Your Expedition

 Fleshing out "Navigating the Terrain," we give explicit directions on how to enter this new career: Decide on a destination, scout the terrain, and decide on a path that is right for you. Of course, the answers are not the same for everyone.

Landmarks

People have different needs at different ages. "Landmarks" presents advice specific to the concerns of each age demographic: early career (twenties), mid-career (thirties to forties), senior employees (fifties) and second-career starters (sixties). We address not only issues such as overcoming age discrimination, but also possible concerns of spouses and families (for instance, paying college tuition with reduced income) and keeping up with new technologies.

Essential Gear

 Indispensable tips for career-changers on things such as gearing your résumé to a job in a new field, finding contacts and networking, obtaining further education and training, and how to gain experience in the new field.

Notes from the Field

 Sometimes it is useful to consult with those who have gone before for insights and advice. "Notes from the Field" presents interviews with career-changers, presenting motivations and methods that you can identify with.

Further Resources

Finally, we give a list of "expedition outfitters" to provide you with further information and trade resources.

Make the Most of Your Journey

The business of making films and television is, in many ways, a business like any other. You have to have knowledge and skill to do well, and you have to work hard to get ahead. At the same time, it is a very different sort of enterprise than most because it deals in the magic of storytelling using visual media. Plus, the industry offers glamour and excitement as writers, actors, and other creative individuals come together to produce major motion pictures, independent films, commercials, sitcoms, dramas, and a host of other projects. It is hardly surprising that so many people want to be involved in the film and television industry.

No doubt about it, a lot of skill combined with a little luck, perseverance, and hustle can land you a job in "the biz," sometimes with a big paycheck attached. True, the bulk of people who work in film and TV, from prop builders to producers, do not make the megasalaries of top actors and directors, but many earn good wages doing what they love. In fact, because many jobs are union positions, paychecks can be quite comfortable. On the downside, the entertainment world is very competitive and work can be sporadic. So, if you do pursue this path, it pays to have a passion for entertainment to drive you on through the tough times.

Another reason so many people want to get into the film and TV industry in some capacity is because they suspect what is, in fact, true: This career can be a lot of fun. While the daily grind of deadlines and creative battles can be stressful, the devotion to artistry and intensity of collaboration generates excitement. Whether you are an unpaid intern, department production assistant, director, or producer, professionals in this field contribute to a final work that may be viewed by millions and even become a part of cultural history. Even a runner ("gofer") on a Harry Potter or James Bond film can feel charged up working on major motion picture.

At the same time, keep in mind that the work is not always lights, camera, action. In fact, filming can be tedious, with a lot of time spent standing around as directors discuss a change in plans, solve problems, or decide on a different approach. When it is time to do your job though, you have to be ready. Often, millions of dollars are being poured into a production, so employers will not tolerate those who cannot meet the daily challenges and perform their assignments with the utmost skill and professionalism. You have to get to work every day looking forward to the demands that are going to be put upon your knowledge, talents, and skills. Although a set may be already built and costumes ready, they may have to be redone entirely because of a last-minute change in the script. Problems like this come up all the time, so you have to be someone who gets excited by creative solutions and working with the team to come up with answers.

So how do you break in? That can be a hard question to answer because everyone who is successful will tell you that there is no one set way to go. For every "rule" about how it is done, there are dozens of exceptions. People will tell you that you will not get anywhere by sending a blind résumé, or cold calling a production office—but then you will hear five stories of entertainment pros who had done just that.

Still, nearly everyone agrees that breaking in is the hardest part. One almost absolute is that you have to have a contact, someone who is already in the business in some capacity, who can lend a hand in getting you that first break. Plenty of people, hearing that, give up before they begin, thinking that they know no one. But chances are, someone in your college alumni association, a friend, a family member, or acquaintance is connected to the industry. If you contact them and say that you are interested in pursuing a new career working in set building, for example, 9 times out of 10, they will be happy to meet and give you advice or recommendations. Bear in mind when trying to meet contacts and get assistance that many people now in the industry got in with help, so they are often ready to help others they know. It is how the business is conducted.

Once you secure an unpaid internship in a props department, then what? Nearly everyone interviewed for this book says the same thing: Whether the project is large or small, in any location, you have to have a great attitude and work extremely hard to get ahead. Many of the jobs in the industry are freelance, everyone moves from project to project, and for the most part, the only way you get a job is via good word of mouth. From your very first day at work, you must start building a good reputation. You want to be the sort of person whom people want to collaborate with. You want to be eager to learn, quick, polite, easygoing, skillful, and fun. Most jobs involve working very closely with other people for long shifts—10-, 12-, and even 14-hour days are not uncommon.

Whether your talent lies in props, art, effects, photography, costume, makeup, writing, or directing, you must be someone who can work well with others, embrace being part of a team effort, and be an open and easy communicator. Even the jobs that involve long hours of solitude, such as editing, writing for film, or scouting locations, will still entail good communications, team-playing, and people skills. An editor must work closely with a director and other members of the team to make the overall vision come to life. A screenwriter meets frequently with the director and production team to make necessary dialogue changes. A location scout has close discussions with the director and production staff to finalize film sites. Then, he or she negotiates with land and building owners to secure those locales. One may think of a storyboard artist or digital compositor sitting for long hours at a drafting table or in front of a computer. This is true, but they still interact with artists and visual effects designers to get the job done.

In many ways, a project is only as good as the team gathered to produce it. This is part of why being a good producer and director is so challenging. Directors like Steven Spielberg, Wes Anderson, or Sofia Coppola have powerful visions, but they must gather a team who can commit to that vision, and who can put aside their own egos to bring that vision to fruition. Good directors assemble a talented crew they can trust and then let them do their job. They listen to the opinions and advice of those on their team. They hire a certain costume designer because they know that professional understands how to reveal a character through clothes. The same attitude applies to the production designer, set decorator, and prop master. You will hear tales of directors who are more like dictators than collaborators. Most of the time, these directors do not last long. You can certainly be demanding, but you still must delegate.

Still, ego does play a role. If you are a director or writer, you need ego to not only have an artistic vision, but put it forward. Even the editors, makeup artists, costumers, and other film and television artists will have distinct ways of approaching their craft that depend on a bit of ego to make the final product excellent. The trick is balancing ego with a collaborative spirit. You can advocate for your vision and style, but you have to compromise and allow for a lot of give and take.

While film and television work depends on having a shared vision, sometimes professionals in this field do not have the same aesthetic. A screenwriter may not share the same view as the director brought on to turn the script into a film. When that happens, they simply have to find a way to work together. To avoid creative conflicts, you may seek out like-minded individuals.

No matter where you are on the job ladder in the industry, you often have to be someone who says "yes." That's not toadying, it is being part of the team. Your job is to make things happen. When someone asks you to do something, you find the way to get it done. Contrasting opinions can make a project more interesting, but employers generally look to professionals to make things happen. Those with an attitude of "Yes, I can do it" will get recommended for other jobs.

A common perception about the film and television industry is that it is ageist. It is predominately seen as a "young man's game," and the word "man" is not too misplaced, either. For example, very few major directors are female. The wider truth is that people of all ages and genders find employment in the industry. A talented set designer is not going to be hustled out of work in favor of someone younger. Nor is it just the established people who stay on. The director interviewed for this book described working on productions with production assistants who were in their fifties—people who were tired of office work and wanted to try something new. Many of them had more energy and drive than the college students working summer jobs. Age is much less an issue than energy. Can you handle the 14-hour days and give your best all from morning to night? Smart people in the industry know that someone who has had a lot of real workplace experience may bring the energy, drive, and cheer needed for a successful production team. Above all, employers seek to hire those who are energetic, enthusiastic, and love what they are doing.

Finally, while ambition is important, it is also necessary to remain realistic. Many people enter an art department wanting to be a production designer, but very few reach that upper echelon. Keep in mind that an art department provides many other positions that are challenging, satisfying, and lucrative. While you may get a foot in the door by taking a mailroom job, only the most aggressive, industrious, clever and talented rise all the way up the industry ladder. It is wonderful to want to be the next Martin Scorsese or head up the creation of fantastical props for a Harry Potter film or design the costumes for an elaborate historical film. But to get ahead, you have to focus on the job at hand and give it your all. Hard work gets respected and usually rewarded, but there is little patience for those who seek to jump ahead without proving themselves in their current positions.

Film and television are constantly changing media with new technologies, new ways of telling stories, and new audiences. The most successful people in the industry recognize and embrace these truths. They also know the history of the industry. After all, the stories and the audiences have always been what it is all about. Exploring the depths of the human experience through comedy, tragedy, or fantasy is what movies and television shows do, and if the idea of being a part of that fills you with joy, then do not let anything stop you pursuing it.

Self-Assessment Quiz

1: Relevant Knowledge

1. How many years of specialized training have you had?
    (a) None, it is not required
    (b) Several weeks to several months of training
    (c) A year-long course or other preparation
    (d) Years of preparation in graduate or professional school, or equivalent job experience

2. Would you consider training to obtain certification or other required credentials?
    (a) No
    (b) Yes, but only if it is legally mandated
    (c) Yes, but only if it is the industry standard
    (d) Yes, if it is helpful (even if not mandatory)

3. In terms of achieving success, how would rate the following qualities in order from least to most important?
    (a) ability, effort, preparation
    (b) ability, preparation, effort
    (c) preparation, ability, effort
    (d) preparation, effort, ability

4. How would you feel about keeping track of current developments in your field?
    (a) I prefer a field where very little changes
    (b) If there were a trade publication, I would like to keep current with that
    (c) I would be willing to regularly recertify my credentials or learn new systems
    (d) I would be willing to aggressively keep myself up-to-date in a field that changes constantly

5. For whatever reason, you have to train a bright young successor to do your job. How quickly will he or she pick it up?
    (a) Very quickly
    (b) He or she can pick up the necessary skills on the job
    (c) With the necessary training he or she should succeed with hard work and concentration
    (d) There is going to be a long breaking-in period—there is no substitute for experience

II: Caring

1. How would you react to the following statement: "Other people are the most important thing in the world?"
    (a) No! Me first!
    (b) I do not really like other people, but I do make time for them
    (c) Yes, but you have to look out for yourself first
    (d) Yes, to such a degree that I often neglect my own well-being

2. Who of the following is the best role model?
    (a) Ayn Rand
    (b) Napoléon Bonaparte
    (c) Bill Gates
    (d) Florence Nightingale

3. How do you feel about pets?
    (a) I do not like animals at all
    (b) Dogs and cats and such are OK, but not for me
    (c) I have a pet, or I wish I did
    (d) I have several pets, and caring for them occupies significant amounts of my time

4. Which of the following sets of professions seems most appealing to you?
    (a) business leader, lawyer, entrepreneur
    (b) politician, police officer, athletic coach
    (c) teacher, religious leader, counselor
    (d) nurse, firefighter, paramedic

5. How well would you have to know someone to give them $100 in a harsh but not life-threatening circumstance? It would have to be...
   (a) ...a close family member or friend (brother or sister, best friend)
   (b) ...a more distant friend or relation (second cousin, coworkers)
   (c) ...an acquaintance (a coworker, someone from a community organization or church)
   (d) ...a complete stranger

III: Organizational Skills

1. Do you create sub-folders to further categorize the items in your "Pictures" and "Documents" folders on your computer?
   (a) No
   (b) Yes, but I do not use them consistently
   (c) Yes, and I use them consistently
   (d) Yes, and I also do so with my e-mail and music library

2. How do you keep track of your personal finances?
   (a) I do not, and I am never quite sure how much money is in my checking account
   (b) I do not really, but I always check my online banking to make sure I have money
   (c) I am generally very good about budgeting and keeping track of my expenses, but sometimes I make mistakes
   (d) I do things such as meticulously balance my checkbook, fill out Excel spreadsheets of my monthly expenses, and file my receipts

3. Do you systematically order commonly used items in your kitchen?
   (a) My kitchen is a mess
   (b) I can generally find things when I need them
   (c) A place for everything, and everything in its place
   (d) Yes, I rigorously order my kitchen and do things like alphabetize spices and herbal teas

4. How do you do your laundry?
   (a) I cram it in any old way
   (b) I separate whites and colors

(c) I separate whites and colors, plus whether it gets dried

(d) Not only do I separate whites and colors and drying or non-drying, I organize things by type of clothes or some other system

5. Can you work in clutter?
    (a) Yes, in fact I feel energized by the mess
    (b) A little clutter never hurt anyone
    (c) No, it drives me insane
    (d) Not only does my workspace need to be neat, so does that of everyone around me

IV: Communication Skills

1. Do people ask you to speak up, not mumble, or repeat yourself?
    (a) All the time
    (b) Often
    (c) Sometimes
    (d) Never

2. How do you feel about speaking in public?
    (a) It terrifies me
    (b) I can give a speech or presentation if I have to, but it is awkward
    (c) No problem!
    (d) I frequently give lectures and addresses, and I am very good at it

3. What's the difference between *their, they're,* and *there*?
    (a) I do not know
    (b) I know there is a difference, but I make mistakes in usage
    (c) I know the difference, but I can not articulate it
    (d) *Their* is the third-person possessive, *they're* is a contraction for *they are,* and *there is* a deictic adverb meaning "in that place"

4. Do you avoid writing long letters or e-mails because you are ashamed of your spelling, punctuation, and grammatical mistakes?
    (a) Yes
    (b) Yes, but I am either trying to improve or just do not care what people think

(c) The few mistakes I make are easily overlooked

(d) Save for the occasional typo, I do not ever make mistakes in usage

5. Which choice best characterizes the most challenging book you are willing to read in your spare time?

(a) I do not read

(b) Light fiction reading such as the Harry Potter series, *The Da Vinci Code*, or mass-market paperbacks

(c) Literary fiction or mass-market nonfiction such as history or biography

(d) Long treatises on technical, academic, or scientific subjects

V: Mathematical Skills

1. Do spreadsheets make you nervous?

(a) Yes, and I do not use them at all

(b) I can perform some simple tasks, but I feel that I should leave them to people who are better-qualified than myself

(c) I feel that I am a better-than-average spreadsheet user

(d) My job requires that I be very proficient with them

2. What is the highest level math class you have ever taken?

(a) I flunked high-school algebra

(b) Trigonometry or pre-calculus

(c) College calculus or statistics

(d) Advanced college mathematics

3. Would you rather make a presentation in words or using numbers and figures?

(a) Definitely in words

(b) In words, but I could throw in some simple figures and statistics if I had to

(c) I could strike a balance between the two

(d) Using numbers as much as possible; they are much more precise

4. Cover the answers below with a sheet of paper, and then solve the following word problem: Mary has been legally able to vote for exactly half her life. Her husband John is three years older than she. Next year,

their son Harvey will be exactly one-quarter of John's age. How old was Mary when Harvey was born?

(a) I couldn't work out the answer
(b) 25
(c) 26
(d) 27

5. Cover the answers below with a sheet of paper, and then solve the following word problem: There are seven children on a school bus. Each child has seven book bags. Each bag has seven big cats in it. Each cat has seven kittens. How many legs are there on the bus?

(a) I couldn't work out the answer
(b) 2,415
(c) 16,821
(d) 10,990

VI: Ability to Manage Stress

1. It is the end of the working day, you have 20 minutes to finish an hour-long job, and you are scheduled to pick up your children. Your supervisor asks you why you are not finished. You:

(a) Have a panic attack
(b) Frantically redouble your efforts
(c) Calmly tell her you need more time, make arrangements to have someone else pick up the kids, and work on the project past closing time
(d) Calmly tell her that you need more time to do it right and that you have to leave, or ask if you can release this flawed version tonight

2. When you are stressed, do you tend to:

(a) Feel helpless, develop tightness in your chest, break out in cold sweats, or have other extreme, debilitating physiological symptoms?
(b) Get irritable and develop a hair-trigger temper, drink too much, obsess over the problem, or exhibit other "normal" signs of stress?
(c) Try to relax, keep your cool, and act as if there is no problem
(d) Take deep, cleansing breaths and actively try to overcome the feelings of stress

3. The last time I was so angry or frazzled that I lost my composure was:
   (a) Last week or more recently
   (b) Last month
   (c) Over a year ago
   (d) So long ago I cannot remember

4. Which of the following describes you?
   (a) Stress is a major disruption in my life, people have spoken to me about my anger management issues, or I am on medication for my anxiety and stress
   (b) I get anxious and stressed out easily
   (c) Sometimes life can be a challenge, but you have to climb that mountain!
   (d) I am generally easygoing

5. What is your ideal vacation?
   (a) I do not take vacations; I feel my work life is too demanding
   (b) I would just like to be alone, with no one bothering me
   (c) I would like to do something not too demanding, like a cruise, with friends and family
   (d) I am an adventurer; I want to do exciting (or even dangerous) things and visit foreign lands

Scoring:

For each category...

For every answer of *a*, add zero points to your score.
For every answer of *b*, add ten points to your score.
For every answer of *c*, add fifteen points to your score.
For every answer of *d*, add twenty points to your score.

The result is your percentage in that category.

Producer

Producer

Career Compasses

As producer, you decide what direction to follow.

Relevant Knowledge of both the business and artistic aspects of filmmaking, as well as people in the industry and the day-in, day-out workings of the industry (30%)

Organizational Skills to manage projects and departments throughout preproduction, production, and postproduction, while also keeping work on schedule and budget (20%)

Communication Skills to put over ideas to financiers and win backing, as well as work effectively with directors, writers, actors, and editors (30%)

Ability to Manage Stress in a job that demands long hours and constant energy (20%)

Destination: Producer

The title "producer" evokes all the glamour and excitement that Hollywood can offer: red-carpet premieres and award shows, the chance to work closely with interesting directors and performers, and of course a high-paying and fast-paced career. All this can indeed be part of the life of a successful producer, but the reality usually involves long hours, high stress, and a lot of micromanaging of complicated finances and clashing personalities. Although the job often pays a lower income than is commonly assumed, you can do very well in this vibrant and constantly changing field if you thrive on risk, challenge, organization, and managing tight and busy schedules. Furthermore, if you are a creative person who is excited about communicating ideas through art and media, you can reap immense personal and professional rewards.

The producer oversees all aspects of a film or show from preproduction to production to postproduction. He or she essentially creates the film or show by developing and approving the script, hiring the director and crew, raising the money to make the film, visiting potential locations to approve them, managing the film throughout its production, and securing its distribution once it is completed. A television producer (also called the *show runner*) keeps a show running smoothly and is responsible for everything from coordinating writers and performers to making sure that the credits are correct. Plus, producers juggle these tasks under extraordinary time pressure.

Most producers do not work directly for a major studio. Rather, production tends to be a freelance job working for or running a small company, which may be based on a studio lot. The studio will then contract this company to produce a film or TV show. Aspiring producers usually begin their careers working for one of these companies as either an unpaid intern or low-paid assistant. Even these positions are extremely competitive and are usually obtained via a recommendation and networking. Sometimes, you can secure an internship through an informational interview. If you admire the work of a particular company, such as Focus Features, look up pertinent names in the *Hollywood Creative Directory*, and ask for such an interview. Through an informational interview, you make yourself and talents known so employers will have you in mind should a position become available. If one does not, but the person with whom you are meeting likes you, he or she may recommend you to someone else.

Of course, if you have the funding, you may be able to head up your own production company without starting at the bottom, especially if you have access to a talented team who can bring your vision to life. Likewise, if you seek out work in a smaller market, as in local television, you already may have skills and knowledge that can garner you a more important job. But generally it is useful to start a bit lower to really learn the whole business.

From being an intern or assistant, the path to being a producer varies widely. You may be asked to read and summarize submitted scripts. If you show some flair for choosing good ones, you may become a development assistant, then executive, then assistant producer. If you are given an opportunity to work on set as an assistant, you can slowly move up to a position such as production coordinator. (Essentially, this is the on-set traffic monitor, who liaises with all departments and assures that everything is going as it should.) Then you might become an assistant producer and eventually producer. Even if you do not perform all these jobs, it is important to understand these roles. Then when you are heading up a team, you know who is essential at every level.

Essential Gear

Never leave home without business cards. The film and television industry is all about contacts and you have to consider everywhere you go, whether it is the gym, the grocery store, or the gas station, as a place to make a contact. To that end, you must carry your business cards with you at all times. As soon as you decide you are interested in the business, have a set of cards made. They do not have to be elaborate; they can simply list your name, e-mail address, phone contact, and a job title. It certainly helps to have a distinctive image on your cards, but the main thing is you want to be able to hand out your contact information wherever you go.

The trek toward becoming a producer may seem arduous, and while it is certainly long, it is not so treacherous as is assumed. The position is less dependent on training and professional background than it is on experience, talent, creativity, business acumen, and professionalism. Talented casting directors and agents often become producers as well. Although it is possible to become a producer with a background in a non-film industry field, such as business management, most producers start in some aspect of the entertainment industry, such as documentary, business, educational, industrial or government films, or in the music video industry. Increasingly, potential producers travel a career path that starts in short animation and Web-based films. Improved, affordable digital technology has made it easier for aspiring producers to create quality work. They often gain the attention of industry pros by entering their films in festivals and competitions. They also post them on sites such as YouTube and iFilm. Producing a film that shows promise can certainly open some doors. Even if your talent garners critical attention early on, expect a gradual journey to regular work at a good wage.

Whether working on a local commercial, a short informational film for basic cable, an independent feature, or a big-budget extravaganza, good producing demands an ability to deal with many different kinds of people while under tight deadlines. You also need an intimate understanding of every aspect of the filmmaking process and the various departments involved. At every stage, you keep a close watch on the budget. Because even the most carefully planned project will hit snags, if not outright disasters, you must be able to remain calm and think fast to solve these problems. The top producers rely on stamina, calm, control, and mental alertness to guide projects to completion.

While many set off on the journey toward becoming a major Hollywood producer, few ever reach that particular destination. However, the continued growth of network and cable television, online films, advertising, and independent films has provided *A well-made documentary can be an excellent calling card.* rewarding producing opportunities. Many producers have long, successful, and satisfying careers making nonfiction television shows, such as those about cooking or history; feature and television documentaries; television commercials; animated and live-action children's shows; and the popular reality shows.

Because nonfiction films and television shows cost less and take less time to produce than fiction features and shows, they are a common route into the world of production. With reality shows and documentaries, a specialized knowledge of a subject can be more important than experience in the film or television industry. You must be passionate about the story you are telling and determined to tell it well. While the finished product may only end up being its own reward, a well-made documentary can be an excellent calling card into this occupation.

An aspiring producer must learn the Hollywood lingo. For example, day for night is a film technique used to simulate a night scene, and MOS means "without sound." Future producers also need to keep up with everything that is happening in the business. Two main publications, *Variety* and the *Hollywood Reporter*, cover all aspects of the entertainment industry, and producers must read them regularly to know what is going on, what sort of projects are stirring up interest, and what productions are on the horizon. A good producer stays informed about who has been

Essential Gear

Use the *Hollywood Creative Directory*. Few other books will help you get around town as well as the *HCD*. You need to know who has which job and how to contact him or her. Because people change positions so rapidly, you will have to buy a new *HCD* every year, but the expense is tax-deductible and worth it to keep abreast of the industry. Be sure to check *Variety* and the *Hollywood Reporter* for reports of promotions and hires as well.

cast in which production and who the financiers are. If you are hoping to produce a similar project, you could approach these people to gauge their interest and perhaps convince them to back your project.

While wages in the film and television industry can be large and are growing, the spread of piracy has cut deeply into profits. This is problematic for film producers who generally do not earn set salaries, but rather take a percentage of a film's earnings. Although the median hourly earnings of a producer in 2004 were $35, according to the Bureau of Labor Statistics, it must also be remembered that producing is not steady work, and one can go for several months between jobs. Likewise, once a job gets off the ground, you may not see any earnings until its completion.

You Are Here

Your journey to a job as a producer can begin from many places.

Do you live in, or are you willing to move to, Los Angeles or New York City? While work in film or television can be found in several cities around the country, the vast majority of the business is in Los Angeles and in New York. If you are serious about working in the industry beyond local talk shows or news, you must live in one of these two cities.

Are you able to work in a non- or low-paying position for as long as one year and maybe more? Nearly all successful producers start off on the lowest rungs of the industry and work their way up. This can mean working as a production assistant or runner or even an intern on a film or television show. Such work is usually unpaid or pays very little. It involves anything from bringing coffee to whomever asks, to standing at a traffic barricade to make sure no one comes through while shooting is in progress, to fetching and carrying equipment from one department to another. However, it is an excellent means of learning how production works and making contacts. From being an assistant, you will work your way up to the demanding position of coordinator, the person who handles all the on-set traffic and communications and troubleshoots problems. This pays moderately better, although still not well enough to support a family. The next job is line producer (for TV) or unit production manager (for film). Both are very important positions managing all the departments "below the line," such as camera, lighting, wardrobe, art, etc. The slow climb to full producer can feel frustrating, but contacts and experience are the only sure ways to rise to the top, and you must know how to manage all the people in the positions you once held.

Do you have lots of patience and stamina, and are you good with people? You will not be in Hollywood five minutes before you hear stories of top producers who regularly scream, throw tantrums, and even throw objects around a room when things go wrong. These stories, can, unfortunately, be true, but the producers who behave this way tend to be either the ones who are so successful that they can get away with it or the ones who will not last long. On your way up, you will have to deal with a lot of demands and short tempers, but once you become a producer, you will have to stay calm in the face of constant upheaval, placate contrasting personalities, and remain upbeat after long and strenuous days.

Are you quick-thinking and creative? Having a lot of unusual ideas and being able to express them in interesting and engaging ways is key to being strong producer. It is possible to get a show or film off the ground with almost no prior experience, simply because it is a powerful idea and the would-be producer has clearly planned well and understands exactly what is involved in terms of budget, schedule, and overall effectiveness.

This has been especially true with so-called reality shows. A show like *Survivor*, which was an instant cultural phenomenon, was the brainchild of a producer with a finger on the pulse of current society and sensed the show could have a wide appeal with well-chosen contestants.

Once the show is underway, things will change constantly, sometimes every few minutes. The ability to remain calm under pressure and quickly come up with new ideas is a powerful key to success in production.

Navigating the Terrain

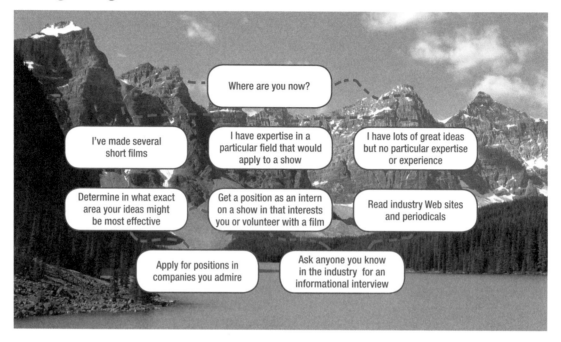

Where are you now?

I've made several short films

I have expertise in a particular field that would apply to a show

I have lots of great ideas but no particular expertise or experience

Determine in what exact area your ideas might be most effective

Get a position as an intern on a show in that interests you or volunteer with a film

Read industry Web sites and periodicals

Apply for positions in companies you admire

Ask anyone you know in the industry for an informational interview

Organizing Your Expedition

Before you set out, know where you are going.

Decide on a destination. Is your heart in film or television? Fiction or nonfiction storytelling? Are you already in a good position to pursue this path in terms of having ability, experience, and contacts? Do you understand film from both a creative and business point of view? Do you have a basic sense of what is involved in creating a film or television show from preproduction through postproduction? Bear in mind that all this will not necessarily get you work. Most financiers and creative people are hesitant to work with anyone who does not have a proven track record, even in the smallest capacity. Be prepared to do a lot of work for free and do not be afraid of starting small. Working on local commercials or educational films can be a useful way of gaining experience.

Scout the terrain. If you are going the route of intern or production assistant to learn the ropes, look for jobs listed in *Variety*, the *Hollywood*

Reporter, and other industry publications. If you are female, consider joining an organization like Women In Film. They will pair you with a mentor in your chosen area, invite you to networking parties and events, hold screenings with the opportunity to talk with the creative team afterwards, and regularly post lists of paying and nonpaying jobs. Special screenings offer an excellent means of meeting people, and in all aspects of the film and television industry, the key to success is whom you know. While you will not be eligible to become a member of the Producer's Guild of America (PGA) for a long time, you can still get on their list to attend some screenings and events. You should also learn the names of everyone who produces work that you respect and wish to emulate. Many people are happy to give advice and will be open to granting an informational interview, wherein you can ask specific questions and opinions and get targeted advice. If they like you, they may make some recommendations, or even pass your résumé to someone who is hiring. You can get contact information for anyone in the industry via the *Hollywood Creative Directory (HCD)*. It is essentially the industry phone book, with names and contact information for all the essential people in production companies, studios, and television shows. If you read about a film going into production that sounds interesting and is being produced by someone whose career you admire, you can contact the production office directly and ask if they need any more unpaid interns. E-mail is often the best means of contacting because people can read your request at their leisure and answer at their convenience. Keep in mind that even unpaid internships are usually obtained via recommendation, and remaining upbeat and persistent opens doors!

Essential Gear

Invest in a set of pretty note cards. It may sound cliché, but if someone's produced something that you think is wonderful and would have liked to produce yourself, send them a handwritten note. It does not matter that he or she does not know you, this is the sort of gesture that might eventually make you a good contact.

Find the path that's right for you. While some producers work in both film and television, the mediums are very different and demand different sets of knowledge and expertise. Before you start putting effort into low-paying work, you should determine which medium is for you. Film

Notes from the Field

Julie Lynn
Producer, owner Mockingbird Pictures (recent credits
include The Jane Austen Book Club)
Los Angeles, California

What were you doing before you decided to change careers?

I was a First Amendment attorney working for a nonprofit. In college, I majored in foreign affairs and theater, so I wanted a job that combined those interests. As a First Amendment attorney, you are constantly dealing with concerns in the arts. I did this for a few years.

Why did you change your career?

As much as I loved my job as an attorney, I ultimately didn't feel the work integrated me enough in the world. I've always loved movies, and I wanted a job that allowed me to combine my abilities regarding creativity, management, and business.

How did you make the transition?

I went to work for a producer. I was a creative executive making $500 a week reading scripts and making notes. When you choose to enter this business from another field, you are going to take a pay cut and a demotion. You just have to expect that. I held that position for a year and a half and then went to work for an independent producer so that I could learn more about hands-on production. I did this for three years and after that founded Mockingbird Pictures. Essentially, any producer who isn't working for a major studio is an entrepreneur.

What are the keys to success in your new career?

The two biggest keys are taste and tenacity. When you start off, you have to put all financial expectations aside and realize that you're going to work for free or very little for a few years. What you want is to find the work environment where you'll be mentored and learn. At the outset, you don't need the most money; you need the best training. As you go on, you gain success by trying to work with people you respect on projects you respect. Taste is subjective, of course, but you have to trust yours. And you find financing wherever you can.

can be more glamorous and, once you get ensconced, better paying, but television offers much more work which can provide you with greater stability. In film, there is an allotted amount of time for the entire production and if you go over, it costs you. A good producer will work 14-hour days, six days a week, during production. Television has a set schedule for a season, and an established show will run fairly smoothly; a single-camera show like *The Office* will take more time than a multicamera sitcom such as *How I Met Your Mother.* Your shortest day will probably be 10 hours. Both paths are very rewarding if you put in the effort, but you should decide which one you want to take before you get started.

Landmarks

If you are in your twenties... Fresh out of college is the perfect age to start a slow climb up the industry ladder, so long as you are prepared to continue living on a low income, working long hours, and doing a lot of grunt work. You may have graduated top of your class in film school and made several student films, but starting off as a production assistant is the only legit position for someone with little to no real experience. However, as a cheerful and hard-working production assistant, you can begin to gain an education in the world of film or television and build a good reputation. Perform well on the job and good word of mouth will get you more and better work.

If you are in your thirties or forties... There is no question about it, Hollywood is very much a youth market and people who come to try their luck later in life will experience some discrimination. This is truer in the area of fiction film, rather than nonfiction film and television. Talent, life experience, a good attitude, and willingness to work hard can often compensate for the perceived handicap of being older than the average beginner in the business. Still, be prepared to start off as an unpaid intern or an assistant.

If you are in your fifties... People with specialized knowledge and an impressive track record in a field that will translate to the production of a film or show have found their way into the Hollywood echelon. A respected anthropologist, for example, with a hook for a science-based

show, may be welcome as a producer. Or a business executive or some-one who has run his or her own business and has a lot of the organiza-tional talents and drive may transfer into a producing career with more ease than others. At the same time, plenty of productions have produc-tion assistants on staff who are in their fifties, raring to go.

If you are over sixty... It is rare, but not unheard of, for people to segue into the film and television world after a long and successful career in a different field. Someone in his or her sixties might do best to team with a younger producer to pitch an idea related to their field of expertise, rather than produce something single-handedly. That would be more likely to acquire necessary backing. As many producers in the business are sixty and over, there is no reason why someone sharp and energetic with a proven expertise could not be a part of that world.

Further Resources

Women In Film is an organization that seeks to promote and empower women in the film and television industry. http://www.wif.org
Filmmakers Alliance is dedicated to the promotion and advancement of independent film and building a strong community of filmmakers. http://www.filmmakersalliance.org
The American Film Institute is a premier national film and television organization, maintaining film heritage, hosting festivals and screenings that anyone may attend, and offering various courses. http://www.afi.com
The Alliance of Motion Picture and Television Producers provides a wealth of information on negotiations and other trade news. http://www.amptp.org/news.html

Director

Director

Career Compasses

Find the road to becoming a successful director of film or television.

Relevant Knowledge of the industry and the tricks to creating a good product (20%)

Caring about the quality of the work and the people involved (10%)

Organizational Skills to manage tight and constantly changing schedules, stay within budget, and keep track of progress in several departments (30%)

Communication Skills to put over your vision, help everyone on set understand what is necessary, and keep everyone in all the departments on the same page (40%)

Destination: Director

When you think of a director, undoubtedly you think of modern greats like Steven Spielberg and Martin Scorsese, or you think of directors as they've been portrayed in movies about the film industry. The 1920s image of a director, with a riding crop and megaphone, is still charming and even appealing. Of course, the daily grind is something far different. For those intrepid enough to undertake the journey, the road to becoming a working director is exhilarating to travel.

Directors do more than tell the actors what to do and shout "action" and "cut." The director interprets the script from the very beginning, mapping out its thematic and visual style before any actors have been cast. Like the producer, the film director is involved with preproduction, production, and postproduction. The director's duties in preproduction tend to involve discussing possible script changes with the writer, suggesting and approving locations, hiring and then planning certain shots with the cinematographer, overseeing auditions and choosing the cast, and organizing the shooting schedule.

During production, the director works long, arduous, stress-filled days during which all the careful plans in preproduction can get upended and changed, often several times in the same day. The director supervises hundreds of people in several departments, like wardrobe, lighting, and set design. This is in addition to *blocking* (or giving instructions on movement) the actors and working with them on their performances, consulting with the cinematographer on shots, and determining when a scene has been shot to perfection and can be considered final. In short, the director is in charge of all technical and artistic aspects of the film.

Furthermore, the director sets the tone of the production. The stress level is very high for everyone involved, and a calm demeanor, good cheer, and positive attitude on the part of the director helps make the shoot more pleasant. Likewise, a director who is easily upset elevates everyone else's stress levels and the project suffers accordingly.

In postproduction, the director works closely with the editor throughout the entire process of cutting the film. More so than an episode of a television show, film is very much the director's medium and the end result must adhere to the director's vision. Thus, long hours are spent over several weeks in the editing room. The director determines if either reshoots or dialogue looping (or dubbing) are required and supervises both.

Scripted television is much more of a writer's medium than a director's, but the writer and director will frequently work together on a show, determining guest cast, locations, and the like. A director's duties in television are less all encompassing than those of a film director, but are done at more than twice the speed. The hours are very long and the days can be taxing.

If you choose to become a documentary director, you probably do so out of commitment to the subject and the desire to tell the story.

Usually documentary directors earn less money than other film and TV directors, so they generally have a passion for their subject matter. Rather than working with actors and a feature-sized team, documentarians work with a streamlined crew, interviewing subjects and researching material. The documentarian has a knack for getting subjects involved and making them feel comfortable on camera. Understanding the technology of filmmaking is important, but being adept at working with people diplomatically is vital.

There is an old Hollywood joke about the number of people who want to be directors. Ask people what they do in show business, and whatever their response is at first, they will pause and add: "But what I *really* want to do is direct." Directing is appealing because no one else associated with the project can claim such complete ownership, and when the film is excellent, the rewards are manifold. It does mean, however, that the road to a job as a director is very crowded with fellow travelers. Whether you have started this journey in your twenties or your fifties, one of the ways to begin to break through, even if you were top of your class in film school, is to start at the bottom as a production assistant. The title "production assistant," or PA, applies to the person who takes care of all the little tasks that are necessary to keep a production flowing—from delivering equipment or coffee to manning a traffic barricade on a street shoot to collecting props after a scene. PAs can be office interns or on-set runners, and they often become a director's go-to person. While the job is non-union, pays very little, and demands a lot of energy and

Essential Gear

Keep DVDs of your short film with you at all times. Before you introduce yourself to anyone in Hollywood as an aspiring director, you must make your short film and then burn dozens of copies and have them handy wherever you go. Burning DVDs is easy and inexpensive. Having your original work marks you as someone who is serious about the career path. Make your DVDs stand out by putting interesting artwork on the covers and labels. Do not handwrite your info on either the case or the disk—even if you are in your twenties, you want to look professional. These DVDs are even better than business cards when it comes to opening doors. Of course, if you find yourself at a party brimming with entertainment notables and you do not have any DVDs, take down names and addresses (or collect their business cards), then mail the DVDs first thing in the morning. Whenever anyone asks to see your work, do not hesitate. It may take them six months to look at it, but you know you have done your part. You can also send a polite reminder card or e-mail following up within a week.

flexibility, it is also a great opportunity to learn absolutely everything about the craft, process, and industry.

While working as a PA you can find out firsthand how film and TV programs are made, you will eventually have to make a short film to prove you have what it takes to make it as a director. Without question, your own short film is the most important career-building tool you can have as a budding director. If you want to direct, it is not enough to think about it, you have to do it, even if you are working a 12-hour day job. The advent of digital film is a boon for aspiring filmmakers because it means making a short is now very inexpensive. You can often get your whole cast and crew to work for free. The exception may be your sound engineer—sound is one of the hardest elements to do well and will kill your film if it is poor. You may have to rent equipment or pay for a location, but these are tax-deductible expenses that will pay off if your film turns out well. Anyone you meet will expect to see an example of your work, and you want to have it ready to show. Furthermore, budding directors should enter their shorts in festivals and competitions. Doing well in a respected festival or competition will definitely garner you contacts, and may land you a job. If nothing else, the cachet of having directed an award-winning film will open doors. You will still need to have a lot of patience and perseverance, but a good short film will get you a long way toward your goal.

You Are Here

Your journey to a career as a director can unfold in many directions.

Do you live in, or are you willing to move to, Los Angeles or New York City? While many successful directors live or do work outside these cities—such as Tyler Perry, Robert Rodriguez, and Ang Lee—the vast majority work in these two cities. Once you are established, you might be able to relocate elsewhere, but while building your career, you will have to be in the heart of the industry.

Are you able and willing to work a low-paying industry job for a year or more? As mentioned, the first job you may land is as a production assistant. The pay tends to be low, no more than $500 a week, the hours are long and your attitude must remain upbeat at all times, even when you are told to be in two different places at the same time. Furthermore, the jobs can be difficult to get. They are often listed in the trades, like *Variety* and the *Hollywood Reporter,* or on online sources like mediabistro.com or media-match.com. But more often than not, even if you just want to intern, you get the position via word of mouth. All projects need low-level assistants, but you typically need a contact who will either hire you or put you in touch with someone who needs a PA. If you are the sort of person who feels uneasy asking people for help or favors, you may want to reconsider a job in Hollywood. Then, once you have proven yourself at one job, it becomes progressively easier to get more jobs and slowly work your way up.

Essential Gear

Collect a diverse DVD library. It is not enough to see a lot of films; a serious filmmaker should be well versed in film history. Much can be learned by watching a well-directed film over and over again, and today's new DVDs often feature instructive director commentary tracks. Even classic films will have commentary tracks from historians, critics, or admiring modern directors. It is worth the money and effort to amass a library of quality films and watch them regularly. Many television shows and documentaries also feature director commentary tracks. Collect your favorites. Nothing beats the experience of learning hands-on, but even if you are not in school, consider yourself a student and watch everything with a critical eye. Knowledge pays. If you are at an event where you meet a well-connected film buff, your knowledge of Truffaut, Sturges, Wyler, and Wilder could advance your career.

Do you have a lot of patience, stamina, and flexibility? The director sets the tone of the project. Every morning, which can start at 5 A.M., the cast and crew look to the director for the outline of the day's work. A scene that may last a few minutes on screen can take 15 hours to establish and shoot, and you have to remain calm, controlled, and positive throughout those 15 hours. Many things can go wrong, from the weather turning stormy in an outdoor shoot to equipment breaking to petty arguments among the cast and crew, and you have to manage all these things. Even on a high-budget film, you cannot afford to lose time, and you must keep everyone focused and committed. Television will also often start at 5 A.M., and the director will work closely with the episode's writer to get the day's scenes shot. An episode will be shot several weeks before it airs, but all the pertinent scenes must be filmed or else the show's continuity will be compromised. It is up to the director to make sure that is accomplished.

Navigating the Terrain

Where are you now?

I have been to film school and have made a short film

I have made a short but cannot decide if I want to be in film or TV

I have recently moved to Los Angeles and have directed local theater

Have DVDs, business cards, and a list of credits available

Ask for informational interviews with assistant directors

Sign up for classes in both film and TV

Apply for jobs as a PA

Work with a writer and crew to make a short film

Organizing Your Expedition

Before you set out, know where you are going.

Make your short film. This cannot be emphasized enough. You do not have to make the film before you start film school or your first low-level job, but you should have some ideas. It helps if you have a sense of what sort of filmmaking you are ultimately interested in pursuing. If you love animation and are hoping to intern at Pixar, do not make a live-action short as your demo, even though that can sometimes be quicker and cheaper. You are better off going in with sketches and ideas to show and discuss if that is all you can manage initially. If you are fascinated with documentaries, find a short story to tell on film. Do not be discouraged if your first effort is disappointing. It is more important to have a vision and real ideas to talk about and pursue.

Go back to school. Film school, that is. Not everyone benefits from film school, but a good one will immerse you in the craft and drill you in technique. The film school at the University of Southern California (USC) is the famous alma mater of George Lucas, Judd Apatow, Ron Howard, Tim Kring, Shonda Rhimes, Bryan Singer, and Robert Zemeckis. The undergraduate and graduate departments are very competitive, accepting few students each year, and you are judged on the basis of your portfolio. (The school does not require you to submit a reel, understanding that not all talented applicants have had the opportunity to create one.) If you are accepted and apply yourself, you are almost guaranteed to go on to be successful. In film school, you have access to excellent equipment, writers, and actors for making the all-important short films that will be your calling card as you make your way through the industry. Furthermore, going to film school will give you the opportunity to make excellent contacts among your classmates and the alumni who regularly come to speak and teach. These contacts are crucial in the film and television industry. Other excellent film programs can be found at New York University, the American Film Institute in Los Angeles, the California Institute of the Arts, and the University of California at Los Angeles.

Decide on a destination. While many directors move back and forth from film to television, most specialize in a field. As you are starting out, you want to ask questions and talk to people in each medium, and if you are on the fence, people will be much less willing to be helpful and take you seriously. Likewise, while many of the same talents and skills are needed in film and television, the process is different, so you will have a better chance of getting ahead if you focus on one area from the outset. Television offers more work, especially with the growth of cable, but it is still often work for hire and the jobs are hard to get. Whichever path you choose, continue to make your own short films and enter them in festivals. This will be personally satisfying and may be professionally useful.

Scout the terrain. Remember you are competing with many others to land directing jobs, but there are also a lot of possibilities. Beyond feature films and network television, new directors find opportunities in documentaries, commercials, educational films, reality shows, music videos, children's programming, exercise videos, and animation. By initially focusing on a less crowded field, you might make more progress. You will also find that the experts in areas like documentaries and educational films can be much more forthcoming with advice and assistance because these fields can be less competitive than other areas of the film and television industry. These professionals will be impressed if you demonstrate a passion and commitment similar to theirs. Combine those qualities with directing talent, and you have the raw ingredients needed to embark on a thriving career.

Landmarks

If you are in your twenties... As long as you are prepared to survive on low wages for several years, this is a perfect time to get into the business. You should certainly consider applying to film school. Film school will give you nuts-and-bolts training, access to excellent equipment, freedom to experiment, and initial industry contacts. In your 20s, you can have some flexibility as you choose your path, and you should try several different options. A summer job as a PA on any kind of project can help you determine your ultimate goal. Likewise, taking the time to make both fiction and nonfiction short films or explore animation might open you to an industry path you hadn't considered.

If you are in your thirties or forties... You should still consider film school. There are plenty of students of all ages and you may find that more respect is offered to those who are not hoping to be hot young things in the industry. Someone who comes to learn the business after gaining some real-world experience is often taken more seriously, especially if he or she has solid ideas, shows talent and skill, and does not expect to be given any special treatment or to work less hard because he or she has already paid dues.

If you are in your fifties... Do not be intimidated by all those who say it is a young person's business. Many industry pros will assure you that there are on-set production assistants in their fifties, many of whom work harder and better than those in their twenties. If you have the stamina to put in the hours and learn the business and make a short film that people like, you can have a successful directorial career. Now in his seventies, Clint Eastwood is considered a brilliant director who gets stronger with every new film.

Notes from the Field
Jamie Schenk DeWitt
Co-President, Easy on the Eyes, Inc.
Owner/managing partner, Silver Lining Films, LLC.
Los Angeles, California

What were you doing before you decided to change careers?

I was an English major and my first job was writing public relations copy. I was interested in magazine writing and was offered a great job for a fashion magazine in New York, but decided it wasn't for me. I did temp work for a while, then went to Boulder, Colorado, and studied poetry under Allan Ginsberg. Then I went to Seattle and worked for a production company that did festival programming, so I was on the booking and business side of the industry for two years.

Why did you change your career?

Something was missing. I wanted to be more hands-on and creative. I'd learned a lot about the business end, but I wasn't using all my energy in a satisfying way.

How did you make the transition?

I started as a PA on a commercial film. That's one of the best ways to start, because you learn everything on the job, even if it is the bottom of the bottom. Then I met a producer who was making an independent film and needed a script supervisor. I didn't know how to do it, but took the job anyway and learned it on my own. The thing is, you have to take these opportunities when they arise, because you don't want to get locked into one job while you're working your way toward where you

If you are over sixty... Again, look at Clint Eastwood. There is no reason to retire and every reason to pursue a dream if you have some patience and can otherwise support yourself. This is an age when you will need to be more focused and set your expectations on a specialized area, like nonfiction shows for cable. If you are coming to the industry late, you should consider how your life experience can best translate into a project. You may make a short film that reflects something of your abilities and experience. You may find you have a different take on a subject than you have seen depicted, and you are the one who can give it verisimilitude.

want to be. If you get locked in like that, people only see you in that position and it's very hard to move on. I found I learned more this way than I would have in school—just working closely with a lot of different people and asking questions and opinions. Finally, I decided to make my own documentary, *Urban Scrawls* (about bathroom graffiti). It won some awards and was seen by some people who went on to really help me. I felt it was something I *had* to do, but you need it if you're going to be a director. You simply have to have a successful film as a calling card; that's how you get hired. It's so cheap these days, with digital film, and there are so many competitions, that if your work is good, it's pretty easy to get it seen.

What are the keys to success in your career?

Your work speaks for itself. If you want to direct, you have to direct something. A 10-minute film that shows any promise and gets seen at a festival will guarantee some phone calls. Another key is being a good person. You really have to know how to treat people when you're running the show. Things will change minute by minute, and it's noticed if you can't handle it. You can have everything organized and set and it can all go wrong, so you have to be able to roll with that. It helps a lot to surround yourself with good people, and then let them do their jobs! You may be running the show, but it's still a collaborative effort and no one likes a control freak. Having a good attitude is one of the best keys to success. You get jobs via word of mouth. If people like you and speak well of you, and you're good, you will be hired.

The novelty of being an older talent may open doors in Hollywood, and you could find yourself busier than you ever were in your previous job.

Further Resources

IFP (Independent Feature Project) A not-for-profit membership and advocacy organization that supports and serves the independent film community by connecting creative talent and the film industry. http://www.ifp.org

IDA (International Documentary Association) A nonprofit membership organization dedicated to supporting the efforts of nonfiction film and video makers throughout the United States and the world. http://www.documentary.org

USC School of Cinematic Arts One of the oldest and best film schools in the nation. University of Southern California also has a range of summer programs that are slightly less competitive. http://www-cntv.usc.edu

Assistant Directors Training Program Co-sponsored by The Directors Guild of America and the Alliance of Motion Picture and Television Producers, this is a highly competitive program for which you must have a bachelor's or associate's degree or two years of experience. You must complete a written exam and other assessments. Graduates are eligible for membership in the Directors Guild and can usually secure jobs as second assistant directors. http://www.trainingplan.org

Writer

Writer

Career Compasses

Get your bearings on what it takes to be a successful writer in film or television.

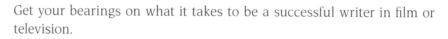

Relevant Knowledge of the subjects you write and the ins and outs of marketing your work (40%)

Organizational Skills to plot and structure a script whether it is for a half-hour sitcom, three-hour epic film, or a 10-part miniseries (30%)

Communication Skills to pitch your work successfully to agents and producers (20%)

Caring about doing good work, even if you find it gets changed radically once it's greenlit for production (10%)

Destination: Writer

The old stereotype of the writer is a man (usually) working long, hard, lonely hours, hunched over paper or a typewriter, ink-stained, sweating, drinking too much coffee, and smoking too many cigarettes. Today, the vision of a writer's life is much less grim. Writers, both men and women, often set up a laptop in a coffee shop, sit in an overstuffed chair with a mineral water or a strong latte within ready reach and start to create. No matter where they ply their trade, writers put in long, often solitary hours. However, if you have a busy, creative mind and a gift for writing snappy dialogue, you may be able to transition into this career without first doing unpaid work or slowly working your way up the ladder. You just need a lot of perseverance and some luck.

Some writers work in both film and television, but while the same talent is needed for both, they require different skill sets and even different mentalities. As with many jobs in the industry, it is best to have an initial focus on the area in which you wish to work. You may have an opportunity to change later, but when starting out, you should be on a specific path.

The film writer works alone or with a partner. When breaking in, you have to have your original screenplay in hand, which is also called a spec script. Actually, if you want to push ahead with getting an agent and meeting with producers, you should have two scripts to show. One great script is great, but having two shows that you are not a one-trick pony, that you have the ability and commitment to finish products, and that you might be worth taking a chance on. Agents enter into a partnership with you for the long haul and want to be assured from the outset that you are worth their effort.

You may be talented, but can you create a script that is going to get you an agent? A spec screenplay follows a rigid format, and if yours does not comply, it will not get read. Fortunately, the formula is easy to learn. Numerous books explain how to write screenplays (Robert McKee's books are well regarded), and many schools offer classes on the basics of screenplay writing. One key to becoming a successful writer is to write continually, and good classes will force you to churn out work regularly. You should also invest in screenwriting software—such as Final Draft, ScriptWare, or SceneWriter Pro—that automatically puts your script in the correct format.

With very few exceptions, a writer must have an agent to get a script read by producers. There are hundreds of agents and agencies, from the large well-known companies like CAA, ICM, and William Morris, to smaller "boutique" agencies that may only represent 20 writers. When you are ready to approach an agent, you should consult books such as *The Writer's Guide to Hollywood Producers, Directors, and Screenwriter's Agents*, which gives information on what a specific agent might be looking for. You do not want to send a romantic comedy script to an agent who specializes in police dramas.

Securing an agent is only half the battle. A good agent will send your script to producers, and you may get called in for a meeting. Most of the time, a producer just wants to talk to you and get the sense that you are someone they can work with. Sometimes, they will option your script. This means that they pay a comparatively small amount of money to secure the rights to the script, although it may never get made. However, being optioned puts you a step ahead of other aspiring writers. A writer with an optioned script is one whose work other producers will want to see.

Usually, your first job as a screenwriter will be as a writer-for-hire. You will either be asked to rewrite a script, for which you may not get credit, or you will be hired to adapt a book into a screenplay. You will have strict deadlines and be asked to do a lot of revisions, about which you will be allowed almost no leeway, but your career will be underway.

Essential Gear

Keep your treatments handy. Your treatment, the one-page story synopsis of your script, is a must for any occasion where you might be meeting contacts. If a producer wants to meet with you about one script, bring treatments for all the others in your arsenal because if you mention one and he or she is interested, it is ideal to hand over something the producer can read at his or her leisure. It can look tacky to carry your scripts around, but having a one-page synopsis with you looks organized.

A television writer's life is much less solitary. Many shows have staffs of around 15 writers who meet in a conference room every day, or at least several times a week, to discuss the various storylines at several stages of production. One writer is assigned a particular script, and then he or she is given a week or so in which to produce a draft, which is then read by the show runner (producer) and writing staff. Once changes are suggested, the writer rewrites the script and then it may undergo more changes. By the time the television script is ready to be shot, the writer is expected to be on set during the whole of production in case more changes are needed. Television is much more of a writer's medium than film, and the schedule, though busy, remains constant. The workday can require long hours, and filming can be stressful as the production team hustles to meet deadlines. A television writer must maintain a good attitude, think quickly, articulate ideas well, and juggle many character arcs and stories at once. The job demands constant communication with fellow writers, directors, actors, and producers. If you crave the sort of writing life that involves holing yourself up in your room all day, television writing is not for you.

Furthermore, you might often have to open up about your personal life. On *Sex and the City*, the writers had to share stories about dating experiences that could become plot points or funny scenes. Even a fantasy show like *Buffy, the Vampire Slayer* asked its writers to share real stories from high school that could give a supernatural story a basis in reality. The best television scripts come from people's real-life experiences, and you have to be willing to discuss them.

There are a few paths to becoming a television writer that do not involve having an agent first. One is to secure an internship. The major networks and a number of production companies all offer internships. Anyone may apply, but competition is fierce. Another way is to get a job as a writer's assistant. These jobs are usually found via word of mouth, although you can write to a show you like and ask if there are any assistant jobs for which you might be considered. Again, the competition is enormous and the jobs are very difficult to get. If you do land one, be prepared to work very hard for long hours at little pay. Your duties will involve everything from basic assistant work, like answering phones, filing, copying scripts, and maintaining calendars, but most writer's assistants are also expected to be in the writers' room during meetings taking extensive notes, which then need to be typed up and organized. This can take hours and you may be at it till 2 A.M. several days a week, and expected to be on the job again at 9 the next morning. However, you will not only get an excellent education in television writing, but, if you do well and people like you, you may be offered the opportunity to write for a show.

There are many jokes about writers being abused in Hollywood—working long hours and not getting the money they deserve. Some are based in truth, but the fact is that, so long as you can put your ego in check, a talented, dedicated, and hardworking writer can enjoy a long and satisfying career.

You Are Here

Your journey to a career as a writer begins with a love of stories and language.

Do you live in, or are you prepared to relocate to, Los Angeles or New York? Established screenwriters have the luxury of living anywhere in the world. If they are needed for a meeting, the production company may fly them in specially. But writers trying to break into the business, especially if they want to work in television, must live in one of the two industry cities. Nearly all the agents are in these two cities, as are the production companies, and if someone wants to meet you, they expect that you be available to meet on short notice. Likewise, as you begin working, you need to be within a reasonable distance to come in for emergency meetings and script consultations. While it is true that a lot of business can be conducted via the phone or electronically, and a writer is less important on the set than anyone else involved with production, you still need to make face-to-face contacts to get your career going. That is why it is vital to be in a city where contacts can be made.

Are you a creative, flexible, and quick thinker? This is more crucial in television, rather than film, but you can be in meetings with agents or producers who might ask unexpected questions, such as "Is there a particular children's book you like that you think would make a good film?" While it is OK to say you cannot think of something offhand, it is better to have a suggestion or two, even if nothing comes of it. Agents and producers want to work with writers who are brimming with ideas. Even if your script is being shot, if an actor or director wants a line change, you should still be able to come up with a few suggestions then and there. They may ask you to take an hour or even a day to refine it, but a quick mind is valuable in Hollywood.

Do you have specialized knowledge of a unique subject or field? Plenty of writers who work on crime or medical dramas do not know anything about the subject and that is OK because professional consultants are on set to ensure accuracy. If you have a background in forensics in addition to your writing talent, you are going to be a very desirable candidate for that sort of show. Likewise, if you have written a spec script about an archeologist solving a mystery and people learn that you are an archeologist, it gives you a hook. More people will want to meet you and read your script, and they will remember you later. You do not always have to write what you know to get ahead in Hollywood, but when you know something that not a lot of other people do—although they may want to—you are at least guaranteed some good meetings.

Navigating the Terrain

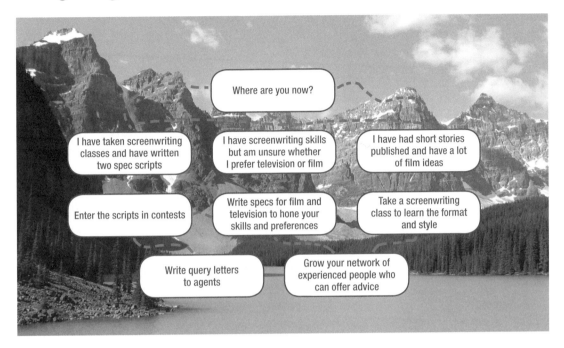

Organizing Your Expedition

Before you set out, know where you are going.

Decide on a destination. It cannot be emphasized enough that, at the outset of your career, you must be focused on either film or television. You may have heard stories of people who had a feature spec script that made the rounds and ended up garnering the writer a television offer. This does happen. Likewise, it is useful for an aspiring television writer to have an original feature-length script to show if asked. But since each medium requires different skills and are difficult to break into, a writer with focus will have an easier time. You can certainly be flexible and prepared to work in whatever area pays you first, but feeling strongly about a specific form will make you a stronger candidate for a job. Producers will always be more interested in someone with focus and determination.

Stories from the Field
Diablo Cody
Screenwriter
Los Angeles, California

One of the hottest new screenwriters in Hollywood also made one of the most unusual career transitions. Diablo Cody wrote the screenplay for the movie: *Juno.* The movie was an enormous hit at the 2007 Toronto Film Festival and became a smash hit at theaters across America. Cody won the 2007 Oscar for Best Original Screenplay. Her story is the stuff of movies themselves. She first worked as a typist and then as a stripper before she became a full-time writer. She freely admits to being an unusual stripper, punctuating her routines with screaming ninja kicks and then writing about the life on her blog.

It was that blog that changed Cody's life. Funny, cheerfully crude, smart, and with a distinct and current tone, it caught the attention of talent agent/producer Mason Novick, who spent several months trying to convince Cody that he was legitimate. He eventually landed her a deal to write a memoir about her life in the skin trade: *Candy Girl: A Year in the Life of an Unlikely Stripper.* He also encouraged her to write a screenwriting sample he could use to persuade a studio to let

Scout the terrain. The film and television industries are quick-changing businesses. There are always new major players and new trends. If you are lucky enough to be a quick writer, it is good to pay attention to the trends and write accordingly. For example, know that when a certain genre of film is released and becomes a monster hit, other studios will be looking for something similar. So if a ghost thriller or kids' fantasy epic tops the charts against all odds, you might try writing something in that genre. Likewise, when trying to break into television, write a spec script for one of the most popular shows on television, choosing your sitcom or hour-long drama accordingly. You may write a wonderful spec based on a show almost no one watches, but unfortunately, you will find that no one will want to read it. Prospective employers want to look at scripts based on shows to whose popular or critical success they aspire.

her write the screenplay adaptation of her book. The result was Juno, a smart and quirky comedy about a pregnant teenager's decision to give her baby up for adoption. The script was so good, Novick sent it out and quickly scored a director and cast. Cody went from writing in the dining area of a Target in suburban Minnesota to being one of the most courted writers in Los Angeles.

One key to Cody's appeal and strength as a writer is that she is able to create three-dimensional teenage girls who are far more real than those who usually show up on television and in movies. Many of Hollywood's top young actresses look to Cody as a hero because she is writing roles that are genuinely interesting to play. Her latest teen comedy script is in production and two others are in development. She was also handpicked by Steven Spielberg to write the pilot for a comedy about a woman with multiple personalities, which is being produced by Showtime.

Cody keeps herself grounded and sharp by regularly meeting with two other established female screenwriters, Dana Fox and Lorene Scafaria. The three plan to start a production company focusing on projects about real women leading real lives. Cody is also thinking about making yet another career transition—she would like to try her hand at directing.

More simply, if you write a spec based on the hottest show on television, everyone will know the show and will be better able to judge your ability to write to characters' voices. Never, ever, write a spec for a show that is no longer on the air. You may have an idea for the greatest *Seinfeld* that never was, but no one wants to read a spec for a show that is off the air.

Enter contests. Almost every week, new writing contests spring up offering prizes ranging from cash to readings by agents. Entrance fees can be hefty, but if you are a finalist in a well-regarded contest, that can open a lot of doors. Do your research before entering a contest, because a number of terms may be attached. Some of the better contests include the Nicholl Fellowship, Scriptapalooza, and the Chesterfield Writer's Film Project. There are hundreds of others. If you have a feature script in a particular genre, you might look for a contest strictly for that genre, such as family, science fiction, or horror. Doing well in a good contest will make you more desirable to agents, who in turn will have an easier time marketing you and your work to producers.

Essential Gear

Cards, cards, cards. A stash of good business cards is a must at all times. Try to create one that has a bit of individuality. This is especially so if you have a unique background that you are bringing to your work. The archeologist who writes mysteries might print up cards displaying his or her name and something like "Digging for Truth" with a picture of a shovel—these are the sort of things that will make people remember you. Furthermore, have some attractive blank greeting cards at hand to send little notes to contacts on a regular basis. If you read in *Variety* that someone you met six months ago just made a big sale, write and congratulate him or her. Perhaps that person will not remember you off-hand, but these little actions can have big dividends down the road.

Take classes. Even the best writer can benefit from some specific classes in the art of screen and television writing. If you are in Los Angeles, you should consider classes through UCLA (University of California, Los Angeles) Extension. Scores of colleges, universities, and film schools offer scriptwriting courses; some are even Internet-based and can be taken from home. Consider taking at least one or two evening classes a quarter. UCLA and other schools have excellent teachers, many of whom currently work in the industry. Classes provide a good opportunity to share your work in a constructive environment. In addition to introductory courses, look for lessons that zero in on very specific areas such as sharp dialogue, well-constructed scenes, and character development. You should also consider taking an acting workshop as a way of understanding and improving your dialogue. Even if you only create period pieces, natural dialogue that flows well is crucial to a successful script.

Landmarks

If you are in your twenties... This is the ideal time to be honing your skills. The trade papers regularly feature stories about a writer in his or her twenties who landed a six-figure deal, but they are the exception.

Your time now may be best spent taking classes, writing nonstop, and learning the craft. You are desirable as either an intern or a writer's assistant and probably have the energy to work for someone else for 15 hours and then focus on your own projects for a few hours more.

If you are in your thirties or forties... A little bit of life experience is desirable in a writer. Agents and producers are interested in someone who has had some other jobs and a varied background from which to draw on. A certain amount of age discrimination may make you less desirable as a writer's assistant, but if you have got some intriguing scripts, which have perhaps placed well in contests, and show a lot of enthusiasm and flexibility, you can still build a successful career in the industry.

If you are in your fifties or sixties... The nice thing about being a writer is that, until you are called in for a meeting, you are being judged strictly on your talent. Again, you will have to rise above age discrimination, but Hollywood can be more flexible than is commonly perceived. Ultimately, good scripts are desired and if you have a fascinating background and talent, you stand just as good a chance of developing an exciting new career at this stage in your life as someone fresh out of college.

Further Resources

MovieBytes   An online publication with a regular newsletter listing contests and opportunities. If you subscribe to its Who's Buying What feature, you learn which agencies and managers have sold what and to whom. The contests page is very thorough and also provides feedback from participants. http://www.moviebytes.com

***Creative Screenwriting* Magazine** One of the best screenwriting magazines with an excellent Web site, this resource is especially useful for writers living in Los Angeles, as they host regular screenings of new movies and have writers and other members of the film's creative team come to talk and do a Q&A afterwards. They also sponsor the yearly Screenwriting Expo, where writers can take classes and have the opportunity to pitch to agents and executives. http://www.creativescreenwriting.com

Broadcast Engineer

Broadcast Engineer

Career Compasses

Guide yourself into the world of broadcast engineering.

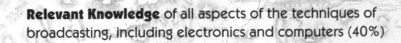

Relevant Knowledge of all aspects of the techniques of broadcasting, including electronics and computers (40%)

Caring about the process, the equipment, and the endless possibilities in a constantly evolving field (20%)

Mathematical Skills for the ability to work with antennas, transmitters, and other complex broadcast equipment that require measurements and various (20%)

Ability to Manage Stress in a job that involves strict attention to schedules and details while working with equipment that requires constant maintenance and care and can often experience glitches, which must be solved immediately (20%)

Destination: Broadcast Engineer

You can be making the most amazing television shows ever—shows that will rivet audiences and change the world, but they will not get anywhere without a broadcast engineer. This is the person whose technical expertise makes broadcasting possible.

Broadcast engineering comprises electrical, audio, and computer engineering. These skills apply at both the studio end and the transmitter end. Almost all television stations will have a broadcast engineer either on staff or as a contract engineer (freelancer). This is more common in smaller markets. Additionally, the transmission may not take place from the studio itself. When a newscaster reports a story from a location, the engineer receives the transmission from there and sends the signal back to the studio and out to the viewing public.

In addition to the management of the transmission, a broadcast engineer will install, maintain, modify, operate, and repair the equipment and systems. The broadcast engineer assures that programs are transmitted at exactly the right time and at the highest quality. Workday details will include the maintenance of the broadcast automation systems for the studio and the automatic transmission systems for the transmitter plant. An engineer must check that the radio towers are always current in terms of lighting and painting. The engineer must also manage problems of signal interference. As broadcasting increasingly goes digital, new facilities are created, new antennae built, and an engineer must be as knowledgeable of the principles of digital transmission and satellite broadcasting, as well as analog systems.

Essential Gear

The address and calendar of your local SBE. Whether you join or not at this stage in your career is not important, but as with every other job in the entertainment industry, good relationships help you secure work. Local Society of Broadcast Engineers (SBE) chapters are usually very welcoming, and you will quickly find yourself with the necessary mentors and contacts. At the meetings, you will learn of innovations in the industry and upcoming events, all of which can be very helpful.

Digital audio and video uses non-linear editing and signal processing, making those systems cheaper and more efficient. The mixing consoles are also going digital, as is the storage system. Digital technology allows effects processing and television graphics to be done more easily and look better. While many people in smaller markets still deal predominately with analog, digital is taking over so rapidly that everyone must become adept at this technology if they are to stay in the field.

An aspiring broadcast engineer should have in-depth electronics knowledge and experience. Most of the work can be learned on the job, but even starting as an unpaid intern at a television or radio station, you must come in with some electronics experience, knowledge, and ability.

The nature of the job tends to vary from place to place, but other tasks that may be involved on the job include the design and set up of audio and video circuits, the manufacture and repair of hardware and software, regular testing and maintenance of technical facilities, and the set up and monitoring of audio and visual links. Other duties include maintaining specialized equipment for satellite transmission and interactive media, troubleshooting technical faults, determining alternate means of dealing with equipment failure, keeping at the forefront of knowledge of new techniques and equipment, custom-making systems for individual programs, and setting up and operating of links for outside broadcasts.

In a small media market, an engineer may work alone, but most of this work is done in a team environment and with regular liaison with other people at the studio involved in the broadcast. A successful engineer must also take direction well, facilitate requests, and work effectively with a team. It is also useful to network and maintain industry contacts. Colleagues should be seen as friends, not competitors. If questions or problems come up, these are people with whom you can work. You want them to be eager to tell you of new technologies.

Most broadcast engineers will work in television or radio, but there is also work in film, video, and sound recording. The competition for positions in major media markets is very stiff. You can expect to work evenings, weekends, and holidays. Some formal education in broadcast technology, electronics, or computer networking is very helpful.

A number of other jobs are related to broadcast engineering and support the work of the broadcast engineer:

☞ Audio and video technician. This person sets up and operates the AV equipment (microphones, sound speakers, video screens, projectors, video monitors, recording equipment, connecting wires and cables, sound and mixing boards, and whatever else is required for the event).

☞ Broadcast technician. This professional sets up, operates, and maintains equipment regulating signal strength, clarity, and range of sound and color. He or she also operates the control panels that select the program's source and will operate the switching from one camera or studio to another, from film to live broadcast, or from network to local programming.

☞ Sound engineering technician. This person operates all the equipment that records, synchronizes, and mixes music, voice, and sound.

In a smaller studio, a broadcast engineer may be expected to perform many of the above tasks. Even if someone specializes in a larger studio, he or she may still be expected to have to take on different tasks under special circumstances. The titles can be quite fluid as well, with "operator," "engineer," and "technician" being used to describe the same position.

Most of the time, engineering work involves being indoors in a controlled environment, but engineers assisting in broadcast news spend time outdoors in a variety of weather and sometimes dangerous conditions. Engineering often requires physical labor. When doing maintenance, engineers climb poles or antenna towers. They often lift heavy equipment to set up a remote broadcast.

Essential Gear

Your amateur radio license. This and your experience in local radio are vital to securing even an unpaid internship. People want to see that you are serious, that you have been working on your own to learn and develop skills. This is one field where a hobby can translate into a fun career, but you need to show that you are committed.

Broadcast engineering is one of the few jobs in the film and television industry that can be done in shifts. However, shifts can include nights, weekends, and holidays because the show must always go on. You can put in a regular 40-hour week, although an engineer in a smaller market may work longer.

While on the job, the pressure to maintain top quality and meet exact broadcast deadlines is immense. Even in the digital age, an engineer must be hands-on to assure that a show begins at the precise second it is scheduled to broadcast. If the TiVOs of millions of viewers miss the beginning of a broadcast, complaints may flood a television station and the engineer will be out of a job. Chief engineers can expect to be on call in the same way as a medical doctor because with programming 24-hours a day, seven days a week, even the most state-of-the-art studio can have something go wrong and problems must be solved at once.

For someone who has a deep passion for electronics, computers, and the inner workings of television and satellites, broadcast engineering is an exciting field where the work is always challenging but fun.

You Are Here

Your journey to the world of broadcast engineering begins with a fascination with electronics.

Do you have strong electronics and computer skills? These days, you must have a combination of both to break into and remain in broadcast engineering. Some aspiring broadcast engineers set up their own ham radio stations or become heavily involved in their college radio and television stations. Some tinker with build-your-own radio kits. All are great ways to gain hands-on experience. If you need to build broadcast engineering skills, you should take some courses or even sign up for a training program at a technical school or community college. In fact, if you want to end up as a chief engineer at a major station, you will need a full college degree in engineering.

Are you endlessly curious and do you love a challenge? A successful engineer is someone who is constantly exploring the possibilities in current and developing technologies. People who are on the job constantly strive for ways to improve broadcasting with new methods of handling broadcast and perfecting systems. But even the most tried and true methods will experience malfunctions of some sort or another. The best broadcast engineers thrill to the challenge of troubleshooting a potential disaster under almost impossible time constraints. The switch to digital has made certain processes easier and less expensive, but new technologies still pose their own challenges.

Are you friendly and quick to ask questions? Engineers are a tight-knit group who love their work and take it seriously. If you are a newcomer who shares that respect and enthusiasm, seasoned broadcast professionals are more likely to give you their advice and assistance. Even if you have a degree in engineering, you should defer to the knowledge and experience of those in the business. Take every opportunity to ask long-time broadcast engineers about the daily grind of the job or any technical questions you might have.

Navigating the Terrain

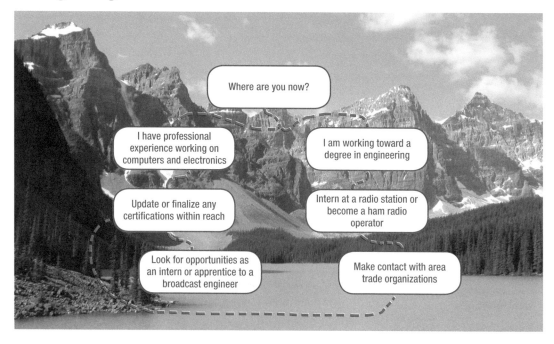

Where are you now?

I have professional experience working on computers and electronics

I am working toward a degree in engineering

Update or finalize any certifications within reach

Intern at a radio station or become a ham radio operator

Look for opportunities as an intern or apprentice to a broadcast engineer

Make contact with area trade organizations

Organizing Your Expedition

Be fully prepared to start the journey.

Go to meetings at your local SBE chapter. The Society of Broadcast Engineers (SBE) has a chapter in every media market, and nearly every professional engineer in the country is a member. You do not have to be a member to go to meetings, and you do not even have to be employed in the business yet. If you are new to the career, much of what is discussed at an SBE meeting will be incomprehensible. Still, you will be welcome if you are friendly and show genuine interest and a desire to learn and progress. You may find yourself with a whole group of mentors, many of whom will be willing to share their knowledge and even assist you in securing an apprenticeship. Established in 1964, the SBE also offers certification for those who master specific technologies.

Get your ham or amateur radio license. As old-fashioned as it may sound, ham or amateur radio is still a valuable way to learn the fundamentals of radio communications and equipment. Plus, amateur radio operators can support their communities with emergency and disaster communications. The more you understand about the technology, the more desirable a candidate you will be for even unpaid intern work. Because engineers are often inundated with requests for training and assistance, they are only going to devote time, attention, and effort to someone who shows aptitude, interest, and dedication. The more you have done to prepare yourself, the more likely it is that a professional will agree to guide and teach you.

Learn as much about the different specialties as you can. As noted, if you work in a major media market, you may end up working in just one specialized aspect of broadcasting. Likewise, if you work at a studio in a smaller market, you may be expected to undertake a variety of broadcasting tasks. Either way, you should take the opportunity before you start to really climb the career ladder to at least understand the basics of the various specialties. This will help you select a specialty that best matches your interests and abilities. Some people specialize in audio consoles, transmitters, or antennas. Knowing at least the basics of how all these technologies work will make you a valuable asset in any company.

Keep abreast of all the technology. If you want to be in broadcast engineering, you are probably already curious and constantly experimenting with how things work. Even if you have a degree in engineering, the best broadcast engineers are the ones who maintain their childlike obsession with how things work. You are eager to experiment and learn. You may know a transmitter inside and out, but you retain your fascination with its workings and constantly play with it.

Landmarks

If you are in your twenties... This is your ideal time to be gaining experience in local radio and television stations. You should take the time to hone your skills and find your strengths and keenest interests, while also making an effort to improve your weaknesses. If you can manage it, you should take unpaid internships in more than one specialty as a way of learning on the job where you might be best suited.

Notes from the Field

Thomas R. Ray, III CPBE
VP/corporate director of engineering,
Buckley Broadcasting Corporation
President NYC Chapter of the SBE
New York, New York

How did you get started in broadcast engineering?

I had attended the Connecticut School of Broadcasting and in my se-nior year of high school, I met the production engineer of WDRC and started sending him tapes to critique. I became a bit of a pest, but when they had an opening for someone to run the Sunday morning public service block of programming—I got it. That eventually led to my running the board for remote broadcasts. I did a lot of other things at the station—repairing outside lights, changing bulbs, painting walls, fixing the roof. The chief engineer decided I had an aptitude for the technical side and gave me little maintenance duties, like cleaning tape heads and calibrating transmitter control meters. He advised me to go to his elec-tronics school. I took a two-year program and got an associate's degree in electronics with an emphasis on communications. I also obtained my third-class license (which was then required by the FCC) so that I could work on transmitters and antenna systems. I then went for a bachelor's degree. In my third year, the assistant chief engineer position at WDRC became available, and I was hired. It was a lot of fun, but also a baptism by fire.

Why did you want to get into broadcast engineering?

I grew up near the studios and transmitter of WDRC. My dad knew the nighttime DJ and we would occasionally hang out at the studio when he was on the air. I was always fascinated by the glowing tubes in the AM transmitter not far from the studio door. I originally wanted to be a DJ. Then I started becoming fascinated by how things work, par-ticularly electronic things. Then I discovered audio production. I started in production, then moved into the tech area.

How did you break in?

As noted above, I met someone and did whatever they needed—cleaning labels off of tape cartridges, painting walls, fixing the roof, cutting grass, shoveling sidewalks, coming in at 4 D₽ 1on snow days and taking school cancellation calls. It was a good education. I got a good fundamental education in the ways of broadcasting and the etiquette required for working in the broadcast environment. I wasn't afraid to work, I wasn't afraid to ask questions, and I wasn't afraid to try something and fail. Well, except something critical and expensive, like the transmitter. I didn't want to smoke that by accident.

What are the keys to success in your career?

You need to have the desire to work your tail off and see it as fun. This is one of those rare jobs that is in your blood and becomes part of you. The business is constantly evolving and you need to keep learning. Those who do not embrace change in this business generally do not survive. I do not consider it a good day at the office unless I either learn something new or can look at something in a slightly different way because I have been enlightened in some way and on a different level. You need to be flexible. Unfortunately, we may find that those who are resisting the conversion to digital transmission may be out of work—once again, you need to be flexible. You need to enjoy making things work. You need to love a challenge. You need to enjoy solving mysteries, as you sometimes need to dig around to figure out what is causing a particular problem. You need to be broadminded. I've walked into stations using computer automation, but they were using a 1950s transmitter. That's quite a technology difference, and you need to know your way around [equipment from] many eras. Get involved with a college or LPFM (Low Power FM) radio station. They always need volunteers. See what goes on behind the scenes. Get to know their engineer. Many of us like having someone tag along once in a while. Call your local station and see if the chief engineer can spend a few minutes with you talking about the business. Most importantly, prepare to enjoy yourself. I am having a great time!

If you are in your thirties or forties... If you have been doing work that either involves computers or electronics, and you have some skill in both these areas, you should determine your best strengths and seek an apprenticeship that focuses on one of those strengths. Get involved with the SBE and work on getting certifications.

If you are in your fifties... If you have a history of amateur radio experience and good computer skills, you may be eligible for an assistant job and can bypass the apprentice route. It will still be appreciated, however, if you approach the field asking for an apprenticeship. If you're coming from an electronics or engineering background already, your skills may vault you into a higher position at the outset. Still, humility and eagerness to learn on the job will be noted and respected.

If you are over sixty... Look for a mentor at your local SBE who is in your age range. If you have appreciable skills and the right attitude, people will be willing to help you find an appropriate place to start a new career in a field that you and they love.

Further Resources

The Society of Broadcast Engineers   In addition to being a great place to begin learning and meeting people, the Web site also has a place for a résumé bank and a job board. http://www.sbe.org

The National Association of Broadcasters   The Web site for the NAB is a great source for resources, events, news, and general information. http://www.nab.org

***Broadcast Engineering* Magazine**   An online magazine with newsrooms, reviews of current products, a variety of technical information, and a job board. http://broadcastengineering.com

Script Consultant

Script Consultant

Career Compasses

Guide yourself to a gig as a script consultant.

Relevant Knowledge of the subject on which you are advising (60%)

Communication Skills to be able to advise in a manner that is easily comprehended, even if the subject matter is complex or arcane (20%)

Caring about the subject, which will be respected and appreciated by those you are advising (10%)

Ability to Manage Stress because your ideas may not always mesh with the producer, director, or writer, and while arguments can be productive, they can also be extremely stressful (10%)

Destination: Script Consultant

There are two kinds of script consultants. One is the person who sets up a shingle as a professional assessor of screenplays, usually for aspiring writers who are desperate to get a foot in the door. For a fee, the consultant will read the script and give detailed feedback on story, dialogue, character development, and structure. Many of these consultants have actually had extensive experience with screenplays and help new writers markedly improve their scripts. A number of them work in the film and television industry in some way.

The other type of consultant, also called an advisor or technical advisor, lends professional expertise to a script so that it might achieve verisimilitude. All the legal, medical, criminal, and forensics dramas on television have script consultants on staff who were or still are professionals in their respective fields. Every show is different, but in general consultants work with writers to help make a story more accurate. Some shows, like the medical dramas *House* and *ER*, have several consultants on staff with different specialties. Depending on the nature of the script, the consultant can work in several ways. The writers may get information on a particular issue from the consultant as they begin to *break* or develop the story. Writers may have an idea, but they turn to the consultants for advice on how to make it work realistically. The first draft of the script is always looked over carefully by the consultant, who then makes suggestions on how to improve it. Occasionally, directors and writers will choose drama over realism, but most shows strive for as much reality as possible.

Essential Gear

Keep business cards with you at all times. Make a set of cards touting yourself as a consultant. Even if you have not done any work yet, you never know whom you will meet and where. You will come across as more serious if you can give a card reminding those you meet of your consulting specialty. They will be much more likely to bear you in mind when they are preparing a new show or film and need a technical advisor in any given field.

Television programs also hire consultants to advise on a single script, or a set of scripts for a story arc. If a show is going to revolve around something specific to do with architecture, for example, an architect will be consulted, usually before the script is written and often afterwards to check for glaring errors. Experts in religion, science, sports, history, art, politics, cooking, geography, and just about any other topic you can think of can all be tapped for script consulting.

Period films regularly hire advisors to comment or instruct on behavior, mannerisms, figures of speech, and customs for a given time period. Writers may contact a consultant during the initial research and writing period. In exceptional instances, a consultant may be asked to be on set during production, especially if the film is based on a real event or person.

Landing your first gig as a script consultant can be very difficult, because 99 percent of the time, you are invited to consult on a show or film when someone involved in the production already knows you. In fact, in the case of Drs. Jonathan Doris and Dolly Klock, the medical script consultants on the sitcom *Scrubs*, their relationship with show creator Bill Lawrence came first. He had been entranced, occasionally appalled, but always amused by the stories his longtime friends told about their lives as struggling med students and hospital interns. From their true tales, the idea for a comedy about young hospital interns was born. Lawrence brought his friends on board to remain as permanent consultants and advisors. They continued to give story ideas, including controversial aspects of medical life—like hungover doctors going around with IVs to keep themselves hydrated. Stories that deal with real issues in medicine in a funny way made the show a huge hit among people in medicine and the viewing public.

Essential Gear

A well-written advertisement. Even if you are not in marketing, a catchy logo and smart copy will make all the difference in attracting potential clients. Anyone can put an ad in the paper giving their name, field, and saying that they are available for consulting work. But if you come up with a catchy slogan or clever copy that pertains to your specialty, you ad is more likely to be noticed, appreciated, and acted on.

Short of having a personal relationship with a show creator or someone else who is involved with the show and has the influence to suggest an expert to hire, people become script consultants who are well known within their area of expertise. The preeminent military historian Stephen Ambrose, for example, acted as advisor on a number of films and miniseries, including the Oscar-winning *Saving Private Ryan*. His book *Band of Brothers* was later made into an Emmy-winning miniseries, and he was available for advice throughout shooting. Professors and other eminent professionals in a given field may also be tapped as consultants.

Someone who is not particularly well known in their field can still become a consultant, sometimes simply by letting the industry know they are available. Setting up a Web site touting their particular expertise, especially if it is unusual, can generate interest. Even old-fashioned advertisements, like in the trade newspapers *Variety* and the *Hollywood Reporter*, can at least garner some calls.

You might also put ads offering free consulting services in student publications at film schools or on Web sites geared for independent filmmakers. If a film student likes your free advice on a no-budget project, he or she may rope you into future projects when they begin working in the industry. Likewise, if the student or short film on which you advise gets recognition on the festival circuit, you will have a credit, which can help you land paid work.

The good news for aspiring script consultants is that, once you have consulted on at least one script, your chances of continuing to work in the field are excellent. The film and TV communities are very small and tight, and producers and directors will always ask their colleagues who they used to advise them on a particular project. If you are easy to work with and a consummate professional, you will be recommended for other productions.

Films need specialists in many areas.

As shows like *Law & Order, CSI,* and other legal and medical dramas and comedies only grow more popular, legal and medical experts will find plenty of work. Other experts should feel encouraged as well because films and television shows involving art, history, and science always need new angles and the specialists to assure accuracy.

You Are Here

Your journey to script consulting begins from an interest in films and television shows about your profession.

Do you have published credits to your name? If you have no personal connections in the industry to begin with, you can build credentials and present yourself as a legitimate consultant in a given field by getting your research published. This does not have to be a major book. You can get published in newspapers, magazines, academic or specialized journals, and online publications.

Do you have a deep passion for both your profession and film? Creative people work long hours in stressful jobs because they are consistently fueled by a passion for the arts. It makes sense that they are attracted to people in other fields who have a deep passion for their work. You can gain respect quickly by showing not just excellence and love in your own field, but knowledge and interest in quality films and shows, especially those that deal with your field in some way. If you can be diplomatic in your criticism of films that have inaccuracies in your subject matter, you will certainly garner interest as a consultant.

Are you patient, sociable, and easygoing? Inasmuch as creators of films and television shows want to truthfully depict a given world, they also want to take the easiest and often least-expensive route to the finished product. A consultant who is too much of a stickler for details and argues a point with no clear understanding of the necessities or realities of filming will not be asked to consult on another project. A consultant may have to deal with difficult people who are in a hurry and just want a quick confirmation of a fact. Someone who can manage temperaments well and explain something in a clear, concise, and comprehensible manner—preferably with warmth and humor—will find themselves in demand.

Navigating the Terrain

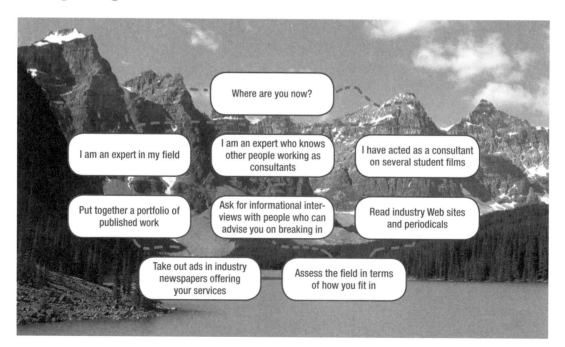

Organizing Your Expedition

Before you set out, have all your gear in order.

Build a Web site. Unless you are a professor emeritus, major author, or otherwise famous in your field, as an aspiring script consultant you should have a Web site that touts your knowledge, experience, and abilities. While preparing your site, you should first do some free advising on student, short, or independent films so that you can then list these projects on your site. Do not be afraid to get into detail. Talk about the film's subject matter and why your consulting was important to the overall strength of the story. Detail all your activities as consultant, and why your particular background and abilities made you such a good advisor. Whereas a professional résumé should be concise, dry, and accurate, a Web site should really tout yourself as a potential script consultant. You want to get producers, directors, and writers excited about working with you. Enthusiasm, balanced with respect for industry and obvious expertise, will get people interested.

Write a blog. Increasingly, well-written blogs generate interest and attention. The screenwriter Diablo Cody got her break because a talent agent/producer came across her blog, liked it, and contacted her to talk about expanding her writing talent into screenwriting. Your blog can be part of your Web site and can discuss aspects of your profession. If your style is warm, funny, and engaging, people will want to work with you. One note: You should be careful about heavy criticism of inaccuracies in shows. Be mindful of your wording. You do not want to come across as snide or pretentious. Try to keep it light, gentle, and humorous.

Ask the locals for help. While producers and directors can be hard to contact if you do not have an in, your own colleagues can be far more accessible. For any show or film, you can look up the consultants and advisors easily on the Internet Movie Database (http://www.imdb.com). You can then send a letter or e-mail to them in care of the show, getting the address from either the show's Web site or the *Hollywood Creative Directory*. If you are in the area where the show is filmed, like Los Angeles or New York, you can even call and leave a message. E-mail, however, is best because it allows people to get back to you at their leisure. When

Notes from the Field

Beth Seltzer
Script consultant
New York, New York

What were you doing before you decided to change careers?

In college, I majored in anthropology and did summer internships involving film and video. After college, I went to California and began working on socially conscious documentaries. I did this for five years, during which I gradually felt I needed a more hands-on way to be socially active and improve people's lives. I was accepted at medical school and am still working as a medical resident in addition to consulting.

Why did you change your career?

I found I missed being in media. Furthermore, I realized from my reading and conversations that a lot of people do not understand medical information and their bodies. I saw that I could combine my media skills and medical knowledge to help people better understand medicine and write about it more effectively in fiction and nonfiction scripts. I also thought it would be fun!

How did you make the transition?

Two ways. One, I learned that there was a residency rotation at Discovery Health that would allow the resident to help create medical education programs for broadcast. I saw this was an excellent opportunity and, even though I already had other plans in place for that summer, I was able to change them and do this rotation. I continue to work for Discovery in a freelance capacity. Sometimes I help create scripts for a medically oriented show, but other times I'm given a written script to fact-check or clarify, or I'll review a show for accuracy. This is very important, because medicine is constantly evolving. When nonfiction shows are broadcast for the general public, they must be absolutely accurate

they do, ask for an informational interview (if that was not the stated reason for your initial contact). Explain that you want to get into consulting and ask them how they did it and what advice they may have. Most people understand that this is a good way of getting in if you do and up-to-date. It's also important to make sure that the shows are not just factually correct but also entertaining, so that they fit the style and brand of Discovery Health.

The second way I transitioned was from my work as a consultant in fiction. I have a number of friends who are writers, and they started asking me for advice on medical situations in their novels and scripts. I realized that there was a need for non-established writers to obtain reliable (and affordable) information, so I made some business cards and started a Web site where I offer free advice about basic issues, like where you can find good medical information online. I also have a blog where I'll discuss medicine in media and incorrect information. Finally, I have a space where people can arrange to contact me for more specific advice and in-depth consultation on a sliding price scale.

What are the keys to success in your new career?

Advertise, advertise, advertise! Let people know you are interested in consulting. Never say no. I've stayed up all night finishing projects on tight deadlines. This lets people know I'm always available and that if they ask me to do something, it will get done, and get done on time. Networking is crucial. When I meet people involved in any arts capacity, I always let them know what I do and give them a card. Be tactful—especially if you see a network program that has an error, you don't want to suggest someone was careless or not trying to do a good job because no one likes to work with a know-it-all. You want to create a safe space for people to ask questions and feel like they'll be respected when they get their answers. Finally, you have to have a sense of humor and understand that sometimes fiction is fiction, and the story has to work. As long as you've been clear that something is not medically correct, you have to be okay with the writer keeping it in the story. In the end, it's their story, and you don't want to fight with your clients.

not know anyone. Some of the best consultants are regularly asked to be involved on more projects than they have time to manage, and you may get lucky and get a recommendation. Luckily, your position as an established professional will speak for itself, and you will be on your way.

Landmarks

If you are in your twenties... If you think consulting is something you'd like to do regularly, make yourself available for free on student and independent films while building up your professional credentials. Concentrate on writing articles and other projects that will act as consulting credentials.

If you are in your thirties or forties... This is the perfect time to branch out into consulting, as you will be seen as having worked long enough to gain some expertise but still brimming with enthusiasm for both your work and entertainment. However, you may not be deemed experienced enough for shows like *Law & Order* that demand seasoned experts, so you may have to labor for free on smaller projects.

If you are in your fifties... You are in the absolute prime position for consulting, as you are probably recognized and respected in your field and have a body of work to point to as backup for anyone who questions your expertise.

If you are over sixty... Again, you are an ideal consultant, having many years of experience to lend weight to your advice. Because you are still active in the field and up-to-date on materials, you can lend a lot of nuance and history to discussion of a subject. Production companies will admire your credentials and appreciate knowing that you are ready to stay with them for the long haul, rather than go back to your field full-time.

Further Resources

The ***Hollywood Creative Directory*** Published every year, this is the book listing the names of the production team on all the television shows, as well as the names of people in every production company in Hollywood. An aspiring script consultant should send their information to every show for which they think they could work. Available at all major bookstores and via Amazon.com.
American Screen Writers Association This organization for screenwriters has a page specifically for script consultants.
http://www.goasa.com/scriptconsultants.shtml

Editor

Editor

Career Compasses

Get your bearings on what it takes to break into the field of editing.

Organizational Skills to keep track of dozens of reels of film and dozens of takes of various scenes. You also need to be good at maintaining a strict schedule (40%)

Relevant Knowledge not only of editing, but of sound, music, directing, and acting (30%)

Communication Skills to work well with the director, sound editor, music editor, and anyone else on the production team who might be involved in perfecting the final product (20%)

Caring about the work, because you will spend many long hours alone with the footage and you have to be dedicated to the process in order to do the job well (10%)

Destination: Editor

On its surface, the business of editing seems basic, and possibly even dull. You take the footage of the show and splice it together in order until it matches the director's intentions. But there is a reason why almost every film that won the Academy Award for Best Picture also got a nomination for editing. Editing is not just a painstaking, meticulous business that requires patience, focus, and minute attention to detail. It is also an art.

The best editors work both alone and with the director to "find the story." That may sound odd, since the film was shot from a completed script. However, as anyone who has purchased DVDs knows, many shot scenes are later deleted. The editor must determine if a scene is crucial to the flow of the story as the film is put together. The scene may be excellent in and of itself, but if it slows the action down, or interrupts a character arc, it does not belong in the finished product. This is not an easy decision, and good editors must not only be able to make that decision, but also communicate to the director why they think the scene must be deleted.

To understand the art of finding the story, look at the story of editing Woody Allen's *Annie Hall*. The initial film Allen had in mind was nearly two-and-a-half hours long, and the story centered more around the Allen character's inability to enjoy life. Editor Ralph Rosenblum, who had worked with Allen several times before, found that the scenes that dealt with the Allen character's relationship with Diane Keaton's character were the strongest. He pared the film down to 90 minutes, and Allen agreed that this was the perfect story. The resulting film won Best Picture and is ranked number 35 on the American Film Institute's list of Top 100 American Films.

An editor must have a strong feel for the story and be a good judge of acting. Scenes can be shot dozens of times, and an actor's performance will be different each time. It is up to the editor to determine which performance is not only best, but also best serves the emotional heft of the story.

One of the most important keys to good editing is patience. An editor works very long hours, often in solitude, which can mean a great deal of control over the work, but also requires intense focus. Editing a seemingly simple scene of two people eating can be as time-consuming as editing an action sequence. The actors will drink water but the glass might be refilled between takes, so that suddenly a glass is full again. Since the performance must come first, strict continuity is sometimes sacrificed in favor of the best scene. (Note: *Continuity* is the visual flow of time and objects, which you do not want to get out of place.) Of course, editing a scene like a car crash, which can involve upwards of 20 shots per minute, is arduous work that can sometimes take days.

In addition to the raw footage, the editor works with the score, sound, and added graphics to create the whole product. On a major film, several other editors get involved in each of these areas, and everyone has to communicate their different needs throughout the editing process. Editing is a great job for someone who likes to work alone, but you still must have good communication and diplomacy skills.

You also need to be able to compromise and take criticism well. A director can look at an edited film and ask that the whole thing be redone, even though weeks have been spent perfecting the product. The director should be open to discussing possibilities, but ultimately, the director is boss, and the editor will have to redo the film per his or her instructions. Sometimes, even when the editor and director agree, the results of test screenings prompt more editing. Producers and studios may put pressure on the team to re-edit a film. Under these circumstances, calm and patience are crucial.

Essential Gear

Final Cut Pro. This is one of the top software tools for digital editing and for practicing at home. While slogging away at an unpaid internship, you will likely not have the opportunity for any hands-on work, so you will have to develop skills in your off-hours. If you can get experience with Final Cut Pro, you will build essential talent for professional editing.

The most common path to becoming an editor, whether or not one goes to film school, begins with an apprenticeship to a senior editor. Although some simply have a strong eye and take to it quickly, most editors build their skills and knowledge gradually by working with others in the field. An apprentice may be in that position for five years or even longer. From there, he or she becomes an assistant editor, and then the best advance to the position of full editor.

Securing editing work is not just about building a respected body of work, garnering skills, and developing talent, it is also about making contacts. Directors want an editor whom they trust with their "baby," someone with whom they can easily communicate and work with comfortably and consistently. Many directors use the same editor on every one of their films. Multiple Oscar-winning editor Thelma Schoonmaker met Martin Scorsese when she was taking a summer course in film editing at New York University, and she helped him with some student films. She has since edited every single one of Scorsese's films since *Raging Bull*. Developing a connection with a director can make for a happy, productive, and stable working life.

Aspiring film editors can teach themselves the basics or take unpaid internships to begin their education, but it is very useful to enroll in an actual course of study. The programs at New York University or the American Film Institute in Los Angeles are very competitive, but if you do get in, you are guaranteed a complete education and a useful springboard for making contacts. Standard coursework for an aspiring editor should include extensive filmography, basic editing, and commercial editing. Because they work closest with directors, film and television editors should understand the directing process. Coursework in direction can be helpful, and you may even try and direct a few plays or films. The editor who understands the principles of direction, as well as the practice and the language, can forge a stronger connection with a director whose work they hope to edit.

This field, like others in the entertainment business, requires that you pay your dues. Be prepared for a long journey with stretches where the work will be hard and the pay low. However, the work can be immensely satisfying and a truly well-edited production is a major achievement that you can be proud of.

You Are Here

The path to becoming an editor starts with a love of the medium and a passion for perfecting a piece of work.

Are you patient, thorough, and a stickler for details? Editing is one of the few aspects of a film or television show in which sloppy work will show immediately and be criticized. While it is understood that mistakes happen, even with the best and most experienced editors, your goal should always be absolute perfection. If poor work on the part of the director, cinematographer, or performers means that you cannot create a seamless scene, you must remain calm and focused and find a solution. Editing requires long hours of close attention, and you have to have absolute commitment to the project down to the tiniest detail.

Are you able to spend several years in school or in on-the-job training that might pay very little? Some people find they have a natural talent for editing, and the advent of digital technology has made it much less expensive and time consuming to teach oneself the basics of editing. However, the reality of breaking into the business is that you need to make contacts, which can often involve taking unpaid internships in editorial departments. Realistically, you should expect to spend several years honing your craft for not much money before advancing to full editing positions.

Are you good with computers and technology, and are you a quick learner? Editing was once solely about cutting up reels of film and splicing them back together to form the cohesive whole. New technology means that much of the work is now done on a computer. (Popular programs are Final Cut Pro, Adobe Premiere, and Avid Express.) Computer editing has made the process much easier in some ways, especially if a scene is to be added back once it has been removed. But it also means that an aspiring editor must have excellent computer skills. You can learn the actual programs on the job. Because technology is constantly evolving, you need to be a fast study. An editor who wants to get ahead needs to show some real technical prowess.

Navigating the Terrain

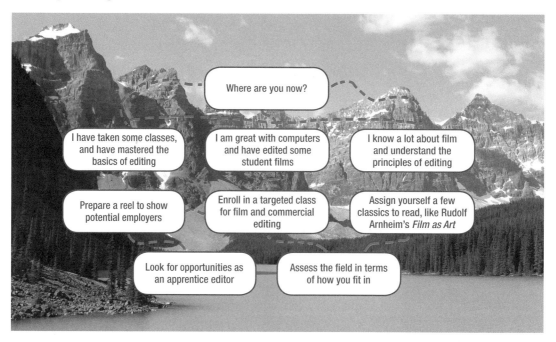

Where are you now?

I have taken some classes, and have mastered the basics of editing

I am great with computers and have edited some student films

I know a lot about film and understand the principles of editing

Prepare a reel to show potential employers

Enroll in a targeted class for film and commercial editing

Assign yourself a few classics to read, like Rudolf Arnheim's *Film as Art*

Look for opportunities as an apprentice editor

Assess the field in terms of how you fit in

Organizing Your Expedition

Have your kit ready before you begin to travel.

Decide on a destination. The basic principles of editing apply whether you are editing a feature film, a television show, or a commercial. The biggest and most obvious difference between the various media is speed. The average commercial is only 30 seconds long and must deliver an impact while not dragging. Likewise, the production time is short and so you must be able to deliver a finished product very quickly, sometimes in a matter of days, depending on the circumstances. Slightly more time is allotted for editing episodic television, although as with all other aspects of working in television, hours are long and time constraints are tremendous. If you end up working on a regular series, however, you get to know the rhythm of the show and the styles of the writers and directors, which can let you to establish a comfortable working routine. In film, you can have months to edit, but the pressure to do good work is enormous. So when starting on the road toward a career in editing, you should have a sense of where you would like to end up. Unlike some other fields, you can apprentice in one area and shift later if the opportunity arises, especially if you learn to edit commercials or television first because it is easier to edit with more leisure. Bear in mind that your apprenticeship may last several years, so you should start in an area where you feel comfortable and have the most to offer.

Essential Gear

A varied demo reel. It is so easy and comparatively cheap now to make short films that you should be able to make a demo reel showing off the versatility of your editing talent. Your demo reel should have several examples of standard scenes, such as action, conversation, dining, romance, etc. You should also have a sample of your work in both a comedy and a drama.

Study editing history. Augment your editing education by watching well-edited films and television shows. If you do not know where to start, look up films and shows that won Oscars and Emmys for their editing. After you have seen the film once, watch it several more times with the sound off. This is an excellent way to study editing and understand what choices

Notes from the Field
Jeffrey Turboff
Video editor
New York, New York

What were you doing before you decided to change careers?

I worked for three years at a television commercial production company as a production assistant/stage manager/assistant to the head of sales. But it wasn't a good fit. I was willing to do anything, but not very good at expected tasks like carpentry and electronics. So they gave me lots of work to do in the video library, until that basically became my full-time job.

Why did you change your career?

I got into editing because I liked it in college, much more than production, which is such an uncontrolled, and often uncontrollable, environment. And I learned that the more I did that had anything to do with editing or other aspects of post-production, the more I felt I was finding my niche. It was something like a gravitational force that pulled me in. Water finding its own level. That sort of thing.

How did you make the transition?

After working at the commercial production company for three years, I was laid off and given a severance check, which I used to take a series of five courses on how to operate an Avid [a commonly used editing machine] The aesthetics of editing I had learned in college as a radio/ TV/film major. So once I got my training, I just called everyone I could find in the industry and asked to work—for free, for cheap, or for full pay. It didn't matter to me at the time, as long as I could make forward progress. It took about four years to really get going full-tilt.

What are the keys to success in your career?

The keys to success are different at different phases of your career. At first you're just trying so hard to get your name out there and build

were made to create the most effective scene. DVD has made this kind of study very easy, as you can pause on an image and do a frame-by-frame forward to view every cut. Try studying the films of Alfred Hitchcock and David Lean. Both directors began their careers as editors, and the skills a reputation. So it takes a lot of persistence and patience. You're an unknown entity, and you have to get people to give you a chance to work on their baby, which, if you fail, may cost them a client, or at least cost them a re-edit. So that's the uphill struggle at the start. And at the same time you're trying to build a good show reel, you may be paired with a producer or director who is making bad choices that can reflect badly on you. So there can be a lot of fighting tooth and nail if you're especially passionate. Some pieces you work on aren't worth that kind of passion. Like nine out of every ten. Save the fighting for that tenth piece. And know that the best thing you can work on outside of the editing room that can help your career inside the editing room is your diplomatic skills. Convince them why you're right. Lead them to come to the same conclusions you came to. Show them why your way works better. Be flexible enough to show it to them their way. and your way. Be honest when their way is not as good. Sometimes they'll insist on their way, even when your way is better. Be willing to give it to them. Pick your battles. You have to be able to articulate why you like one choice versus another. The better you can identify what works and [what] doesn't and develop a vocabulary to discuss it with a producer or director, the more your vision becomes trusted, and that's when you begin to transition from Final Cut or Avid operator to being an editor in the true sense of the word.

Learn something about crafting narratives, both from screenwriting books as well as from editing books. DVD bonus material is a great resource, too. You want as many ways to tackle a narrative problem in the edit room as possible. Flexibility and the ability to think outside the box are key. And remember that concise is almost always better than verbose. Never bore the audience.

they learned in that capacity made an enormous impact on the look, flow, and feel of their films. The famous shower scene in Hitchcock's *Psycho*, is a prime example of the power of editing. The 45-second scene has over 90 splices. When watched slowly, you will find only one shot that shows the

knife entering the body, and this shot features no blood. The skill of the direction and editing is what makes this scene powerful and one of the most terrifying in cinematic history.

You should also, of course, watch films that are poorly edited. Start with films that are considered far too long. As you pay attention, you will start to see where better editing would have improved the film, and you can apply these practical lessons to your own work.

Prepare a demo reel. To become an apprentice editor, you must have some work to show a potential employer. No matter how much you know about film and how impressed an editor may be with you as a person, almost no one will agree to take you on without seeing a sample of what you can do. They will not expect total professional quality (that is why you are asking for an apprenticeship), but they will look for skill, creativity, and vision. You can gain experience and prepare a demo reel by volunteering to work on short films and student films. You can even shoot some film to edit yourself.

Landmarks

If you are in your twenties... Recent college graduates and film aficionados are often in a good position to take unpaid work for a year or more, since they are used to living close to the bone. If you are good with technology and have taught yourself the basics of editing, you might consider trying directly for an unpaid internship in an editorial department. If you do well there, you may be in a good position to seek an apprenticeship.

If you are in your thirties or forties... Someone looking to enter the field of editing after working elsewhere a while should definitely try to enroll in a full study program. This is a useful way to gain the knowledge and skills needed, but also it is a great way to make contacts and meet aspiring directors with whom you might work.

If you are in your fifties... If you have good computer skills and are handy with technology, you may just try to take a short course to learn hands-on editing and the business of editing. Seek out advice wherever you can to meet potential employers.

If you are over sixty... You might be pleasantly surprised by the interest a director will have in you, provided you have the skills and know-how necessary to do the work. It will be assumed that someone a bit older will have even more patience and devotion and ability to focus than a younger person who is perhaps thinking he or she might end up the next David Lean.

Further Resources

American Cinema Editors The professional association of film editors has an excellent Web site with information about student programs, technical innovations, member contact info if you are looking for a mentor, competition information and a tech blog.
http://www.ace-filmeditors.org

***On Film Editing* by Edward Dmytryk** One of the best books on principles and techniques of film editing. Available in bookstores and on Amazon.com.

Tisch School of the Arts at New York University One of the best film schools in the country and the place where Thelma Schoonmaker met and began working with Martin Scorsese. http://www.tisch.nyu.edu

Camera Technician

Camera Technician

Career Compasses

Guide yourself to a career in the camera department.

Relevant Knowledge of the variety of cameras, the way they each work, how to work with light, and how to set up and best execute shots (40%)

Caring about doing excellent work to the best of your ability even under the harshest circumstances (30%)

Communication Skills to work well with each member of the camera team, as well as the lighting crew and the director (20%)

Ability to Manage Stress and still do good work when the hours are long and the shoot physically exhausting (10%)

Destination: Camera Technician

All quality films, television shows, commercials, and videos depend on a good cinematographer to clearly capture the images. While proper lighting and focus are important, what distinguishes the best cinematography is a good eye and an understanding of how to develop a look that will service and enhance the story. Furthermore, the best cinematography is visually arresting and powerful, but is not something that distracts from the story.

The art of cinema is, naturally, visual. Directors want to work with camera technicians who will best capture their vision. Many directors develop lifelong working relationships with directors of photography whom they trust so that they can be assured that their projects will always have the look they desire. Some directors freely admit that it is the brilliance of the filming, rather than the directing, that makes their work so excellent.

To better understand the art of cinematography and the unique relationship between director and photographer, study the films of Swedish director Ingmar Bergman. His director of photography was Sven Nykvist, who is considered by many in the industry to be one of the greatest cinematographers of all time. His interest and emphasis was on simplicity and naturalism. He manipulated light to create moods and show human faces at their most naturally emotive. His naturalism lends scenes an emotional heft. For Bergman, who always wanted to explore the depths of human emotion, Nykvist was a perfect fit. Nykvist spoke of studying natural light and light in buildings as inspiration for his lighting schemes, always striving for the simplest methods possible.

Essential Gear

The *Hollywood Reporter.* If you have just moved to LA and have no contacts but are determined to land at least an internship, pick up the *Hollywood Reporter.* Once a week, it lists the Production Report, which is essentially the industry classifieds. Here you will find every shoot that is looking for team members. Listings provide addresses, phone numbers, and names of key production staff. You can fax your résumé or drop it off in person. Although most jobs are secured via recommendation, many people get their first gig through an ad in the paper.

A camera department consists of several team members, all of whose work is crucial to the look of the finished product. While very few end up as directors of photography (DP), many end up in camera jobs that require skill, creativity, and artistic ability and are personally and professionally satisfying. In addition to the DP, usually about nine members make up a camera team, including a loader, focus puller, camera operator on the main camera, camera operator on the second camera, and assistants for both cameras. The loader, also called the clapper loader, puts the film in the camera and operates the clapperboard that signals the beginning of each take. The loaders also mark the actors and maintain the camera department's records and paperwork. These professionals take on a great deal of responsibility because they are usually the only members of the team who directly and physically oversee the undeveloped negative. They transport the negative to the laboratory for development. Any incorrect or careless handling of the negative at any stage can render an entire day's work useless.

Focus pulling is a major job that requires immense technical skill. Also called the first assistant camera, the focus puller's job is to maintain the camera's focus while filming. Focus pullers are not looking through the camera while working, so they must have an excellent eye and a good sense of the camera and the action in order to do their job well. A focus puller must also have a strong relationship with the camera operator, as they work closely and each person's work assists the other.

A camera PA can move into an assistant job quickly.

The first job most people get in a camera department is that of camera PA, or production assistant. This is grunt work, but it is also absolutely essential. The camera PA does whatever anyone asks and provides whatever is needed throughout the day. During filming, the camera PA stands in what is called "Video Village," the area where the film is shown on playback monitors. Here, the PA watches everything that is going on and communicates it back to the camera team. The work is difficult, but it is an excellent education. A camera PA who is enthusiastic and efficient will move into an assistant job quickly.

Teamwork plays a fundamental role in a camera department. Everyone assists everyone else. Even the DP cannot be governed by ego and personal artistic impulses because he or she needs the work of the camera team to make the director's vision come to life. Additionally, the DP must work closely with the lighting crew and, of course, the film's director. The ability to collaborate, to communicate, and trust is vital to good cinematography.

Camera work on a television show is also very technical and requires skill and artistry, but certain programming is less challenging than others. For instance, in a standard four-camera sitcom, cameras are all planted and once focus is established, little has to be changed throughout a shoot. The work is desirable because it is steady, but someone new to the business should try to be a PA on commercials, films, and single-camera television shows as well to learn how to film under more challenging circumstances. Try to get as diverse experience as you can, including shooting outdoors, which can be more difficult because of weather and other variables.

Unless you are on a regular television show, camera work may mean a lot of travel for shooting on location. Plus, shoots can last up to 16 hours per day, so you need stamina to make it through.

You must be deeply passionate about visuals and the ever-expanding possibilities of cinematography, including digital filming, if you are going to be successful in the field. A camera PA will be hired without experience, but never without the love of the art and technicality of cinematography.

You Are Here

The journey to work in a camera department begins from an interest in motion picture photography.

Do you have a love of photography and a good sense of its possibilities and challenges? Almost everyone who gets involved in cinematography had an interest in still and motion photography from a young age. The popularity of digital cameras and camcorders has allowed much of the general public to take good photos and make little films. The person who is drawn to professional filmmaking gets intrigued by the technicalities and aesthetics of framing, light, and depth and experiments with a variety of possibilities using different cameras. Very different techniques go into the filming of people, landscapes, and moving objects. A basic understanding of what is involved, as well as a fascination with and respect of the process, is necessary for anyone entering camera work.

Are you a good team player and able to put aside your ego for the sake of teamwork? The members of a camera team work their long, hard hours together; if anyone slacks off, everyone else's work and the project itself will suffer. Even on a no-budget project, time and money is wasted if mistakes are made in filming. Everyone on the team must be able to communicate well and collaborate with complete trust. Someone whose interest is solely in forwarding their own career is probably not someone who will be giving their all to the team. If you are working as a loader, which you may do for several years before advancing, you have to love loading, even though in your heart you know you would be an excellent focus puller. Ultimately, being able to collaborate is key to moving on.

Are you able to travel to potentially difficult locations for weeks or months at a time? If you look at the credits of a major film, you will see several camera units, often in different countries. Usually, local crews are used. However, anyone who works in a camera department must be prepared to travel to a location for work. The production will put you up in a hotel or motel, and this will be your home for weeks or months. Location work can be difficult and even dangerous with extreme weather and tough environments. If you are going to pursue this work, you have to be excited by these possibilities and embrace the challenges.

Navigating the Terrain

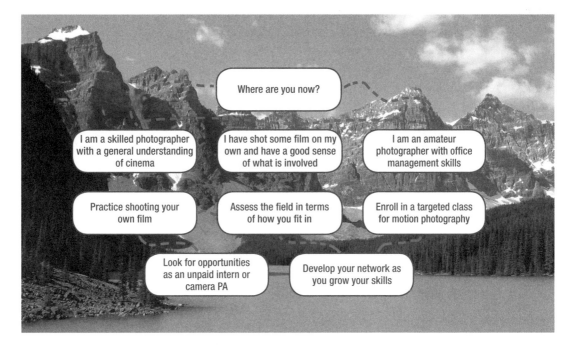

Organizing Your Expedition

Have your kit ready before you begin to travel.

Get a good 35-millimeter camera. Even if you know the basics of photography, you have to practice to maintain and further develop your skills. You will get a good, well-grounded cinematic education as a camera PA, but in your off-hours you should be constantly shooting your own film. You want to give yourself space to experiment, to learn by error, and to really grasp possibilities. Doing this on your own time will put you in the game when opportunities for assisting come around. The more you understand about the intricacies of aperture, light, focus, and speed, the more you can contribute to a camera team.

Be in good physical shape. Camera work can be extremely physical. Whether you are male or female, small or large, young or old, you have to be able to carry heavy equipment. You must comfortably walk and even run with large cameras on your shoulder. You have to be physically fit to lug and set up equipment in rugged terrain, often while wearing a belt laden with tools and extra equipment. If you are working at a high altitude or in heavy wind or rain, you still have to perform as if you were on a soundstage.

Essential Gear

A good camera. This really cannot be emphasized enough. If you want to work in film, you must film constantly. When you are a camera PA on a location shoot, you can ask some of the senior members of the team to come and film with you. Most of them will be happy to work with you and offer advice. They will appreciate and remember your dedication. You should always have your own camera handy, even just to shoot your own "making of" film of the filming.

Take on as many challenges as you can. Even after you begin working as a camera PA, you will have time off between jobs when you will not be earning. This can be the opportunity to get involved with short films where you might get to either do the shooting or at least be an integral member of the team. Look for projects that test your talent and where you will learn new techniques. Shooting action in bright sunlight or tight spaces demands an artistic eye and a lot of skill. Going from a wide angle to a tight focus takes patience and practice. Jump at the chance to operate state-of-the-art equipment, such as a Steadicam, which is a stabilizing mount that allows for a smooth shot. Getting involved in smaller projects will also help you learn to think quickly and outside the box. The most expensive and well-planned film benefits from team players who can make fast decisions and adapt to unforeseen circumstances.

Put together a demo reel. While some people work as loaders their entire careers and are perfectly happy never get behind the camera lens, all positions on the camera team are competitive. Because employers will want to assess your skills and abilities, create a short demo reel of film that shows your range and potential. Your demo reel should be short, yet comprised of a variety of scenes, such as a couple walking and talking, a nighttime shot, a shot in extreme weather, a tracking shot, and changes in angle, light, and focus. You can include as much as you like, but be sure to present your best work and demonstrate your versatility.

Landmarks

If you are in your twenties... Film school is not necessary for a career in camerawork, but this is a good time to take some classes and learn the basics. Film school is especially useful for making those all-important contacts. Directors and photographers often meet at film school and end up working together their entire professional lives.

If you are in your thirties or forties... If you have good experience working in a team environment and a grounding in photography, you might be considered a better candidate for a camera PA than someone in their twenties with no life experience. If you are well-traveled and enthusiastic, you are even more desirable.

If you are in your fifties... You may want to look for work in commercials initially, something shorter that will give you some quick experience. Shorter projects can give you the opportunity to prove yourself and meet people who may be interested in working with you and recommending you to other professionals.

Notes from the Field

Marta Weiss
Camera first assistant
Los Angeles, California

What were you doing before you got into camera work?

My bachelor's degree was in communications, and I filmed my thesis before going on to do a course in anthropology at the Film Center in Santa Fe. I got an MA in anthropology and film, but didn't really know what I wanted to do with it. I'd always liked working with cameras, but wasn't sure if I could turn it into a career.

Why did you get into camera work?

I knew I wanted to do something with photography, but even though I'd been experimenting with still photography since I was 12, it wasn't quite stimulating enough. The day I walked onto a film set, however, the light went on, and I knew that this was it; that this was where I wanted to be, and I had to find a way to stay.

How did you get your first job?

I was just finishing my MA coursework in Santa Fe at a really good time, when tax credits meant that a lot of industry work was coming to New Mexico. A film company advertised at the center and so I went and interviewed for the camera PA job. Long after I got the job, they told me the reason they hired me. They told me what would be involved

If you are over sixty... If you have an excellent demo reel, proven team experience, and a great attitude, you may be able to get good work in television, especially on smaller cable shows where the work is not as arduous, but the need for skilled people with energy and enthusiasm and team-player abilities is enormous.

Further Resources

The Society of Camera Operators   A nonprofit organization geared toward recognizing and nurturing talent in the field, the SOC has a magazine, hosts events, and provides a number of useful links, such as to rental houses and film school programs. http://www.soc.org

with the job and asked if I would be up for it. I answered, "Whatever you'd like me to do, I'll do it." Other candidates talked about their skills and talents, but I was interested in helping the team. They knew that they could ask me anything, and I'd say yes and try to make it happen. I ended up being invited to come to L.A. and work here, which I knew I wanted to do, since it's the epicenter of the industry.

What are the keys to success in your career?

A good attitude. This business is all about relationships and teamwork. The people who are most successful are the ones who get along with everyone. A lot of people are nice, but some can be very nasty, and you still have to find a way to work with them. You really want to be able to say the right things to the right people; it makes a big difference. On any level, you want to be someone without ego, someone who's there to help. You need to be fast, efficient, polite, and have a sense of humor. You don't have to go to film school, but it can help with your overall understanding of the process. However, you're learning on the job, so when you're starting out, try to do a lot of different things and work with different types of cameras and situations. You also want to meet a lot of people. Once you're in the union, you'll be on an availability list when you need a job, but you mostly get jobs because people know you and your work. And you have to love the business. I've loved the work in every position I've had.

Cinematography.com   An online forum for everyone involved in camera from students to DPs, this is a great source for news, resources, asking questions, and getting advice. http://www.cinematography.com

The Cinematography Mailing List (CML)   Featuring discussions on cameras and an open exchange of ideas for professional cinematographers. Beginners are able to post questions. http://www.cinematography.net

Location Scout

Location Scout

Career Compasses

You will always know where you are heading as a location scout.

Relevant Knowledge of an area, of filmmaking, and of all the cost, sound, and logistical considerations involved in location filming (30%)

Organizational Skills To keep track of various possible locations and their advantages and drawbacks as well as all the chosen locations for a project (30%)

Communication Skills To negotiate effectively with land and building owners and explain to the production team why you think this location is ideal (30%)

Mathematical Skills to keep the budget in mind and consider what might be needed to make a particular location work (10%)

Destination: Location Department Scout

From the gas station where the family's van leaves behind Olive in *Little Miss Sunshine* to the great vistas of Middle Earth in the *Lord of the Rings* trilogy, any space—indoors or outdoors—that you see in a film or on a television show that is not created by builders or computers is discovered by a location scout.

On its face, the job is fun and easy. You get to travel on someone else's dime, and all you have to do is find a space that works best for the script. The reality of the job is much more involved. The director and producer usually want something very specific in a location. Finding an available spot that meets their requirements and does not break the budget takes a very specific talent and perseverance. In addition, if it is a long shoot, the location must be near facilities that will accommodate the whole crew.

Scout is a perfect name for this job because those in the field spend a great deal of time traveling and searching for the perfect setting. A director may ask a location scout to find a house to use as an exterior. The description may be simple: two stories, made of wood, a little shabby, ga-

Essential Gear

A clean driving record. Almost wherever you are based, location work will involve a lot of driving. It is not enough to have an up-to-date license; you will not get location work if your driving record has even the smallest blot, because that may involve extra insurance, and few employers wants to spend more money or take that sort of chance. There are courses you can take to reduce points on your license.

rage in the back. Since so much production is in Los Angeles, the scout may typically drive around a few neighborhoods, taking pictures. Because its architecture is so diverse, Los Angeles offers a treasure trove of possibilities. The scout spends several days driving, taking pictures, and making notes. Once the scout targets the ideal home, he or she may get the producer and director to view the house

to make sure it matches the "vision" for the film or TV show. The scout discusses price and scheduling with the homeowner, who then signs release forms formalizing all terms of the production. A homeowner has to be prepared for long hours—sometimes an exterior shoot begins at 7 A.M. and goes till 7 P.M.

Even with an enormous budget, locations must still be easy to access and work with. Several beautiful locations in New Zealand simply could not be used for *The Lord of the Rings* because they were too treacherous. Although all actors and crew are insured, production companies tend to want to spend less on insurance and prevent accidents.

Stories of location nightmares can fill a book. Famous examples include the typhoon that destroyed sets of *Apocalypse Now*, causing a delay of several months; and freak storms (among other disasters) that simply ended the filming of *The Man Who Killed Don Quixote*. The latter can be viewed in the documentary *Lost in La Mancha*. Everything from unpredictable and extreme weather to a sudden war breaking out has ended a production and even sent the entire crew running for their lives. Of course, such stories are the exception, but an aspiring location scout should be aware of everything that can possibly go wrong. A good knowledge of film history and the stories of "locations gone wrong" can help scouts from repeating costly mistakes.

Scouts balance many variables in picking a setting.   A good location scout must have a strong vision and take into account multiple factors. It is not enough to find the perfect patch of woods for a period battle scene, a location scout also assesses costs, acoustics, the means for providing electrical power, and all other logistics for setting up the crew and equipment.

A scout may find a nice bit of woods but then realize that the equipment will not fit in the space, that the lighting is awkward, or that planes regularly fly overhead. Attention to all these various elements is vital to choosing the right film setting.

With tight budgets and other restrictions, location scouts often have to think outside the box. Several scenes in the comedy classic *Monty Python and the Holy Grail* were shot on Hampstead Heath, a very crowded public park in London that is near a noisy intersection. The logistics and sound problems posed a great challenge, but it was simply the best location they could manage for the money.

For most major films, a locations department finds the settings where to film. These departments are headed by a location manager, and the scout or scouts work under this manager. Most location scouts begin their careers working as unpaid interns or low-paid production assistants (PAs). Professionals with related experience may sometimes skip the interning stage. You may have had work coordinating events or managing a crew. If you have handled location matters on a low-budget or no-budget film, your credentials are even more desirable. A location scout who is going to work regularly must have a strong sense of aesthetics, an understanding of the technical and artistic aspects of filming, logistical thinking, financially savvy, extraordinary diplomatic skills, and a passion for challenges and problem solving. Someone who is full of ideas, has an excellent memory, is a bit of an adventurer, is fun to be around and pleasant to work with will nearly always be in high demand.

You Are Here

The path to a life in the locations department begins with a love of movies and an interest in places.

Are you a strong, quick, and creative thinker? Good location work is all about being able to envision possibilities, anticipate problems, and keep all the necessary parameters in mind. You must understand budgets, logistics, light, and weather. You can look at a place and envision the scene or scenes in a television show or movie. You can quickly determine possible problems, and come up with a variety of solutions to those problems. Additionally, when the director and producer look at the location and suggest other possible drawbacks, you are quick in coming up with yet more solutions.

Do you excel at both working alone and working with others? Many jobs in location scouting will involve hours and hours of driving, often on your own. This part of the work can be tedious, especially when trying to find the perfect lonely spot in the middle of nowhere, which requires driving through miles and miles of nowhere. You must be someone whose overall dedication and interest makes these exhausting trips a fun challenge. Additionally, you must maintain focus to find the ideal setting. But whether you are dealing with people who will grant permission for a building's use or discussing possibilities with the production team, you must maintain an engaging, diplomatic, and pleasant demeanor.

Do you love to travel? Most location scouts do not travel the globe, but you have to be prepared for anything. Generally speaking, a producer or director can hire locally based location experts more affordably, rather than send a Los Angeles-based team to scout locations. However, on a big budget film, you may be sent anywhere and everywhere. This can be fun, but be prepared to be sent to places that are dangerous, have extreme weather, or are difficult to navigate. You do not just want to maintain your passport, but also your immunizations. It also helps to have a basic grasp of languages, the ability to drive a manual transmission vehicle on either side of the road, and a knowledge of customs in a variety of countries.

Navigating the Terrain

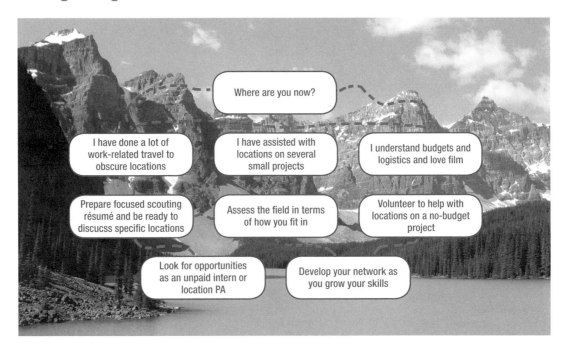

Where are you now?

I have done a lot of work-related travel to obscure locations

I have assisted with locations on several small projects

I understand budgets and logistics and love film

Prepare focused scouting résumé and be ready to discucss specific locations

Assess the field in terms of how you fit in

Volunteer to help with locations on a no-budget project

Look for opportunities as an unpaid intern or location PA

Develop your network as you grow your skills

Organizing Your Expedition

Gather all the tools you need for the trek to the locations department.

Get a good camera and take a photography course. Because you will have to photograph potential film sites from a number of angles and in at least a few different lights, you need some solid camera skills. Some projects may even require that you shoot digital video. If you are not already a serious photography buff, a course can help. It is useful to learn the language of photography, such as "aperture," "diffraction," and "microprism," as well as the logistics of filming. You can learn the exact techniques for photographing locations on the job.

Master negotiation skills. Many location scouts find themselves having to regularly negotiate with land or building owners for the right to use the space. Scouts and property owners need to make an agreement on the extent of the rights and the amount of time and perhaps certain

Notes from the Field

Smokey Forester
Emmy and Peabody-winning field producer
New York, New York

How did you get into location work?

I majored in religion in college and had no idea what I wanted to do. I needed a part-time job, so I went to New York Public Television and they hired me. When I was about to graduate and look for full-time work, they happened to need someone. It all fell into place. I'm a big believer in serendipity. I became a PA on a public affairs show. They had no money, so I could get promoted quickly. I was interested in documentary work, and they were amenable to that.

Why did you want to go that route?

I wanted to be active in making nonfiction shows and films. I was interested in dealing with content. I met someone who worked for the documentary division at NBC and they helped me get a job there.

How can someone transition into location work?

Getting started is the hardest part because you get work by being in people's Rolodexes and via good word of mouth. Forget cold calling and sending out résumés; that's a waste of time and effort. Everyone knows at least someone related to some part of the industry, and they can help you get a position as an intern. Volunteering is good too. If

changes, like painting or planting. Some building owners, especially in L.A. where they can be savvy about the industry, will ask for several thousand dollars simply for the right to use a building a few more hours, or to give it a much more expensive coat of paint than needed. Oftentimes, this negotiation takes place when it is too late to change the location.

Take a course in basic filmmaking. You may not be interested in producing, directing, or cinematography, but one of the best ways to learn filming logistics is by taking a class in the subject. Eventually, you will learn to trust your eyes—when you see a potential location, you will imagine how it will translate to the needs of a specific film. As your career progresses, your knowledge of filmmaking can improve your location skills.

you're a volunteer on a production and do a bang-up job, you will be asked to do more work. You've got to be persistent and cultivate these relationships.

What are the keys to success in location work?

Location scouting is a part of producing. It's a way to save money because someone pre-negotiates with the owner of land or property. You have to be good with scheduling and managing money, but you also have to be a great diplomat. You want to make friends with the owner of that property, so that if shooting starts and they come out and start screaming at the crew to get off their land, you can go and talk to them and they'll remember you and let the shoot continue. You have to find the access road to get to where you need to shoot. Finding where and knowing how to shoot is very important. There is a lot of work to do in prep, but if you do it well, the shoot will go well. You also have to be up-to-date with technology. There's hi-def and video. Everything is changing constantly. You need to know how it all works. It's important to maintain good relations with people, even your competitors. Sometimes work gets farmed out and you want to be one of the people who is asked to help. You want to keep active and in touch. When you're on a job, that's a great time to make social calls and tell people what you're working on. It's very different when they sense that you're calling because you need a job. No matter how successful you are, it's still all about good relationships.

You will develop a keen sense of how the right place can dramatically enhance a story. The lonely and beautiful mountain ridge in the Oscar-winning *Brokeback Mountain* was almost another character in the film. That landscape heightened the sense of sadness and the possibility of love, and it is an excellent example of the location scout's fine work.

Landmarks

If you are in your twenties... Volunteer to be an intern on a variety of different productions. This is a great way to gain a lot of experience and meet a wide assortment of people, which is absolutely crucial to a long and successful career. Most of your work will be freelance and you will get jobs via good word of mouth. Making contacts early will be invaluable later on.

If you are in your thirties or forties... Look for opportunities as a location department PA. Convey to a production company that you are serious about staying in location work. Your dedication to the field can make you a more attractive candidate than someone younger who may be jockeying for another position, such as a second-unit production assistant. Always show that you are knowledgeable and enthusiastic—these qualities are valued in the film and TV industry.

Essential Gear

A good camera. It cannot be emphasized enough that you must be able to take good pictures and keep your own records of what you find. You should be logging all locations you like because even though they may be rejected for one project, they may be ideal for another.

If you are in your fifties... Volunteer on some small and/or low-budget projects and build up a list of credits. If you can show you have the capacity for the work and are quick to learn, you will be a good scout candidate. Experience in a related career such real estate sales and event planning may help you transfer more easily into this job.

If you are over sixty... Become a real expert on the city of Los Angeles or New York, where much of the work for local productions and television is based. Show you have boundless energy, enthusiasm, and a general understanding of filming. These are the qualities of a desirable location scout, especially for low-budget projects that need someone who is reliable and sharp.

Further Resources

LocationScout.com A very good Web site offering job listings, forums, information on the union, technology, and many other useful links. http://www.locationscout.com

Location Managers Guild of America Includes information about location work, a calendar of events, and provides a list of members and contact info. http://locationmanagers.org/cms

Association of Location Scouts & Managers (ALSAM) Features a member directory with contact info, a page of news, and useful links. http://www.alsam.net

Agent

Agent

Career Compasses

Guide your way to a career as an agent.

Relevant Knowledge of the business, what's going on at any given time, and who the major players are (40%)

Caring about your clients and the quality of their work and the quality of the projects you secure for them (10%)

Communication Skills to pitch people and scripts effectively and convince people to say yes and spend the money (30%)

Ability to Manage Stress in a fast-paced, constantly changing environment where the work is hard and the hours long (20%)

Destination: Agent

Actors and writers and even a number of directors and some of the best technical workers in film and television rely on agents to help them secure work and advantageous contracts. Agents predominately work for writers and actors, sending scripts to production companies and headshots and résumés to casting directors in the hopes of getting their client a job. When the client is hired, the agent then negotiates a contract with the production company, wherein salary, working conditions, special benefits, rights, and residuals will all be discussed. When the contract terms are settled, the agent then receives a commission, usually 10 percent of his or her client's salary or fee.

Many in the industry will tell you that the stereotypes and jokes about fast-talking, hustling agents are true. The agent played by Tom Cruise in *Jerry Maguire* is typical, without the personal redemption. To a certain extent, an agent must be tough, brusque, and a little ruthless, because it is an extremely competitive business. Not only does an agent compete with other agents for a small amount of contracts, but also he or she must be a firm negotiator, because companies are always looking to pay a writer or actor the least amount possible. The agent who is strong and yet diplomatic is the one who will do best for his or her clients.

As aggressive as an agent must often be to land good contracts, it is more important that he or she be personable and generous, both with clients and contacts at production companies and casting offices. As with nearly every job in the industry, an agent's depends upon personal contacts. Agents cultivate relationships with producers and directors. Because they know about scripts that are being developed, agents arrange auditions for the acting clients they think may suit the role. Or an agent may have a terrific script, and because of his or her professional contacts, the agent can get it into the hands of directors, producers, and actors who can help get it made. Obviously, there are unpleasant agents whose good sense of talent and negotiating skills catapult them to powerhouse status. They may make deals all over town, but the job is best suited to a strong diplomat whose intelligence, taste, and judgment is beyond reproach.

Aspiring agents must choose their field of interest early, because different skills and knowledge bases are involved in representing actors or writers. The best talent agents are excellent judges of talent. They go to plays and view actor demo reels to find new talent to represent. Agents representing writers love to read scripts and have a good sense of story structure and dialogue. They need to communicate the story simply and effectively to producers and development executives. The agent must also be aware of what sort of stories are garnering interest in development circles and be able to tailor pitches accordingly. A new children's fantasy story will be likened to the Harry Potter series for example. That can make a project much easier to sell.

Most agents get into the field by first working as an agent's assistant, either to a single agent or several agents in a firm. Some agents even begin by working in the mailroom in a large agency, such as ICM, CAA, or William Morris. It is understood that everyone working in the mailroom wants to work his or her way up. To advance, you must be friendly, efficient, sensible, aggressive, and a people person.

Work as an agent's assistant can be very stressful. (Watch the character Lloyd, the agent's assistant in *Entourage*, and you will have some sense.) Duties include answering phones, making calls, filing, writing summaries of scripts, maintaining records, and handling all mail duties. Assistants also read the trade papers, making notes of

Agents are both friendly and aggressive.

relevant announcements and events, and highlighting any mention of all clients. In addition, they maintain a calendar of events, such as awards ceremonies, and sometimes attend those functions. Although assistant work can be difficult and time-consuming, it is the best way to learn the business, get to know people, and develop your all-important pitching and interpersonal skills.

For most aspiring agents, the next step is to move up into a position as a junior agent. In a smaller firm, this will involve assisting the senior agent in an executive capacity and doing much of their duties on a smaller scale. Junior talent agents will go to plays and recommend possible actors to the agent. They will probably handle at least some aspect of a new actor's career, or they may take on the full duties of preparing the actor for casting calls. Junior agents who handle writers will read all submitted scripts and prepare one-page summaries for the senior agent to read. Junior agents will often communicate with new writers at the agency and put together lists of potential places to send their scripts. Sometimes, junior agents approach a development executive with a new script. If the script ends up being bought and is successful, the junior agent's career can skyrocket.

Junior agents who work at a major agency often advance to senior agent within that same agency. Many who prove themselves as senior agents move on to different agencies after a year or two or start their own business. Senior agents at major firms have great industry cachet. However, even they must do business as the company dictates. For some of the most creative agents, this ends up being stifling. If you have a good reputation and strong relationships with a few clients, you may feel confident in setting up your own business. The best agents never forget that the business is all about relationships. You not only need to make good deals for your clients, you need to be someone they can talk to and trust. You want to be the agent your writer or actor will stay with if they become the next Judd Apatow (the director of *The 40-Year Old Virgin*) or Cate Blanchett.

Finally, you have to be able to sell. Ultimately, that is what your knowledge, gift of gab, and good relationships are all about. If you can put it all together to sell a person or a script, your career, as well as those whom you represent, will thrive.

You Are Here

The path to becoming an agent begins with a love for the business and desire to see the best actors and writers get the best work.

Do you know a lot about the real business of the film and television industry, including the names of the movers and shakers? Even someone fresh out of college on their first day in a mailroom is expected to know who most of the major industry players are. You may worry about coming across as pretentious, but you will actually look ignorant if you do not know the names of the presidents and vice-presidents at all the major studios, as well as executive producers of the hottest television shows. Anyone can name major stars, but having a strong knowledge of character actors, rising writers, and mid-level directors and producers will show you are serious about becoming active in the business.

Do you love film and will you see anything and always stay to the end of the credits? A big part of being an agent is going to a lot of films. This may sound like fun, and it often is, but you will be expected to see most of the films released in any given year, not just the blockbusters. You certainly do not have to like every film you see, but you have to see them all and should be able to discuss them a length. Agents who handle television writers and actors are likewise expected to know almost every show on network and cable television.

Are you a people person? Jeremy Piven's portrayal of an agent on HBO's series *Entourage* may make an agent seem devious and self-serving, but he is still a people person with an eye for talent. The best agents genuinely like people and love to meet and talk to anyone and everyone. You have to be as engaging with your clients as you do with the people you want to hire as clients. If you are personable and engaging, you may start friendships and professional relationships with young actors and writers that last throughout their careers. Those personal bonds are priceless. An agent whom clients want to stay with no matter how they high their star rises is an agent who will remain in business as long as he or she wants.

Navigating the Terrain

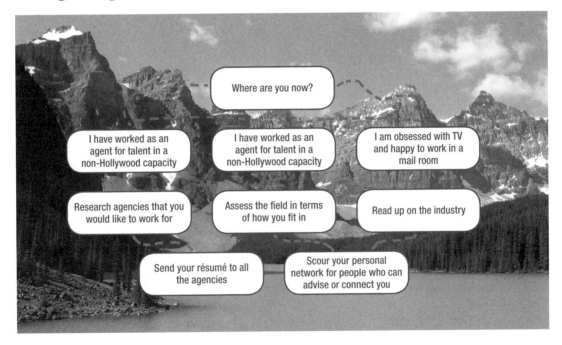

Where are you now?

I have worked as an agent for talent in a non-Hollywood capacity

I have worked as an agent for talent in a non-Hollywood capacity

I am obsessed with TV and happy to work in a mail room

Research agencies that you would like to work for

Assess the field in terms of how you fit in

Read up on the industry

Send your résumé to all the agencies

Scour your personal network for people who can advise or connect you

Organizing Your Expedition

Get everything in order before heading out.

Read all the local papers. Agents must make it their business to know everything that is going on in the industry. While they usually have assistants to summarize *Variety* and the *Hollywood Reporter* to them,

Notes from the Field

Chris Aldrich
Owner, Aldrich Entertainment
Los Angeles, California

What were you doing before you became an agent?

I majored in biomed [biomedical] engineering and electronic engineering at Johns Hopkins, but I've always been obsessed with movies. While I was at Hopkins, I took over and got them to refurbish and update the campus movie theatre. I also convinced them to add more film classes and sponsor more student films. I was co-chair of their film speaking series the same year as the hundredth anniversary of film, and I decided to defer medical school and go to Hollywood.

Why did you decide to pursue this career?

I was having too much fun. I'd built one of the best movie theaters in the U.S. and decided that the next best thing to do would be to produce a movie that would have its premiere there.

How did you land your first job?

I had become friendly with Millard Kaufman, an Oscar-nominated screenwriter who was a Hopkins alum from the class of '39. He'd come to Hopkins to give a lecture on film, and the first movie we showed at the new theater was his *Bad Day at Black Rock.* He knows everyone and gave me a lot of advice. He told me that by starting in a big agency, I could get to know how the business works and a lot of people and transition anywhere after a year. So I sent a résumé to CAA, and they

aspiring agents at least skim these major trade papers daily. They also page through *Entertainment Weekly*, which will have some discussion of the business of the business and entertainment trends, along with profiles of entertainers and reviews. A smart agent also reads the entertainment sections of the *Los Angeles Times*, the *New York Times*, and a summary of the British papers. Many writers and actors who gain success in Britain come to America. Someone who wants to be serious in the business at least knows their names and talents. A person who really wants to make waves reads all the book reviews in the major papers, even if they do not have time to read the books themselves. A interviewed me. The HR woman liked that I had good manners and recommended me as an assistant. Normally, I would have started in the mailroom, but the rules are hard and fast until the company needs to break them. At that time, they needed an assistant, so they broke the rules and I got in.

What are the keys to success in your career?

You really need to work hard. You have to read an immense amount of material—scripts mostly, but also newspapers and books. When I was an assistant, one of the senior agents was looking for a good part for an actress returning from sabbatical. I stayed late on a Friday to type up 20 titles that I'd read and liked. I wrote short summaries of each story and the female characters. That list was circulated and within three years, almost all the films were made, all using CAA stars. You also have to be a smart and social person. You need to do well at parties and be good at managing relationships. Also, and this may sound obvious but it's actually not discussed much, you must be able to sell. That's what you're doing and you have to be able to do it and do it well. You also need to have excellent taste in material. People need to be able to trust your taste. As an assistant, you're basically trying to sell your taste and hard work to your bosses. As an agent, you're selling it to producers and studios. And you need to know the taste of people you are approaching. There will be a number of executives at a given studio and you need to know which one will like the script you have to sell. Relationships are important in this business and you have to develop a lot of trust.

talked-about book will always have movie rights optioned, and more often than not, it gets made into a film. An agent who pays attention to a well-reviewed book long before it stakes a place on the best-selling charts can sometimes land an early deal that will turn into a gold mine. Adaptations tend to be more popular with producers than original screenplays because producers often believe that hit novels have more of a built-in audience and a level of recognition that will attract investment money and a stronger cast. An agent who is aware of what is going on in the world of fiction, and even nonfiction, is one who will be able to make smart deals fast.

Take a public speaking course. If you are interested in becoming an agent, you probably already have a gift of gab. But it is one thing to be engagingly chatty and quite another to be persuasive and commanding while also being warm and friendly. The best agents are the ones who can read people quickly and assess exactly what sort of tone and approach will work best to at least garner their attention, if not secure a deal. A public speaking course will teach you tricks for persuasive speaking and what to do when meetings are not going well, which happens fairly frequently. The grace with which you handle complications and rejection will be as much a measure of your skill and talent as your ability to select good clients and land them good deals.

Learn your film and television history. Do you know the names and plotlines of all the films that ever won the Oscar for Best Picture? Are you aware of all the Emmy-winning television shows? If a young actress is referred to as a "Bette Davis type," do you know what that means? (It certainly doesn't mean anything having to do with Baby Jane!) Plenty of successful agents are not overly familiar with film and television history, but if you get to a place of trying to arrange a deal with a director or producer who is steeped in the history, you must be able to hold your own. Most of the artistic community loves and is proud of its history and responds best to those who share that love and pride. You will look smarter and more serious if you can at least sustain a general conversation about film and television history. It is also very easy to learn. Plenty of books and Web sites cover the history of the Oscars and Emmys in depth.

Landmarks

If you are in your twenties... This is the perfect time to compete for a job in the mailroom. The competition will be stiff, but you are probably in a good position to work hard for very little money for several years, and may not mind feeling invisible or demeaned.

If you are in your thirties or forties... You can still get a mailroom job, and they may appreciate that you are not one of the cookie-cutter twenty-somethings who flood them with applications every day. You may also try approaching smaller agencies for assistant jobs. If you have worked in a fast-paced office, you will be a very desirable candidate.

If you are in your fifties... If you have office experience, knowledge and passion of the industry, and are fun and engaging, you should definitely be approaching the smaller agencies for assistant jobs. Some of the smaller agencies are fairly laid-back and want someone steady who is not afraid of work but is easy to get along with. They may even take a chance and hire you as a junior agent. Those who have developed strong communications and negotiating skills in a career such as law or sales may transition more easily into this field.

If you are over sixty... You should approach single agents. Many agents run a small office virtually single-handedly and want an assistant who is smart, capable, and no-nonsense, but also fun. The pay will probably be low, but you can have more fun, get to do more work, and learn a lot more than someone who is spending two or three years in the mailroom.

Further Resources

Creative Artists Agency (CAA) One of the biggest and most respected agencies in the business. A very good place to send a résumé.
http://www.caa.com

Hollywood Representation Directory A yearly publication listing all the agencies (including CAA) in town with contact information. You can research good agencies to approach by size or specialty.
Available in bookstores or Amazon.com.

Visual Effects Artist

Visual Effects Artist

Career Compasses

Guide yourself into the world of visual effects.

Relevant Knowledge of the various intricate techniques involved in creating powerful visual effects (40%)

Caring about doing excellent work that may take hours to complete a few seconds of finished film (20%)

Organizational Skills to keep track of schedules, changes, budget constrictions, and scenes in various stages of completion (20%)

Communication Skills to work with your team and the director (20%)

Destination: Visual Effects Artist

The Wizard of Oz. Star Wars. The Lord of the Rings and Harry Potter movies. A large part of what makes all these films so effective and memorable are their visual effects. While it may seem as though effects are a relatively new aspect of filmmaking thanks to the advent of CGI, effects have actually been used since film began. Films like 1927's sci-fi fantasy *Metropolis* and the first Oscar-winner, *Wings*, employed effects that continue to thrill modern audiences. Today, effects are used to some degree in almost any film you see as well as in many television shows. A period film may need extra background. A realistic action film may need safety wires removed, or more flames and smoke added to enhance an explosion.

In brief, visual effects involve the creation of special imagery for live action films, television shows, commercials, and videos. An aspiring visual effects artist must have a basic understanding of filmmaking, image making, story structure, and engineering. Because computers are essential to the craft, effects pros master all the latest software and electronics tools. Quality effects go beyond computer smarts, though—they bring together a unique combination of art, technique, craft, and science. Effects artists know the fundamental building blocks of art. They can draw, paint, and sculpt. They can get their visual ideas down on paper. Because some effects are simply better when created by hand, visual artists often build scale models, prosthetics, animatronics, and explosions. In addition, the best artists know how their effects and designs support the storytelling.

Essential Gear

Demo reel. This more than anything is crucial to your first job. You can know all about visual effects, but if you want anyone to hire you, you must have a demo reel that shows the range of your techniques and your ability to work on a variety of projects.

While many visual effects artists learn all this on their own, an art or film school can provide comprehensive training and connections to future employment. An institution such as the Gnomon School of Visual Effects in Hollywood lets students get a sense of what their real strengths and interests are and then provides the lessons to hone visual effects skills. Image-making, rendering, model-making, practical effects, *compositing* (overlaying separate images into a final image), and effects animation all require specific training.

Internships and apprenticeships are still the best ways to learn the craft. Working side by side with experienced people while actually creating something may seem daunting, but for someone who is eager to pursue this field, it is exhilarating. Seeing how it is done, day in and out, will prepare you like nothing else for the rigors of the work. Of course, such opportunities, even unpaid, are still extremely competitive.

Traditionally, people who got into visual effects were interested in "magic" from a young age. The possibilities of creating fantastical images in theater and film fascinated them. The great master of stop-motion animation, Ray Harryhausen, spent much of his childhood in his family's garage, building models and filming them. His obsession began with the original *King Kong*, and he effectively taught himself how to create visual effects from researching the work done on that film. He made his own short films, which he used as a demo reel to eventually land himself a job doing animation for Paramount's short films.

A more modern effects wizard who still uses old-fashioned techniques is multiple Oscar-winner Nick Park of *Wallace & Gromit* fame. He played with design and animation from a young age, developing a unique style and sensibility that helped him segue first into commercials, and then into his own short films.

Would-be visual effects artists tend to play mostly on their computers these days, experimenting with the vast array of graphics and animation programs. Anyone who wants to work in the industry must have a demo reel, a DVD that shows examples of his or her work, to act as a calling card. Whether the demo reel is comprised of scenes or actual short films, this is the only way to put yourself forward. It has become very easy to get short films seen, thanks to YouTube and iFilm and other online sources. John Lasseter, animation giant and head of Pixar, recommends that anyone who wants to be in film in almost any capacity make an animated short. It is cheap, comparatively easy, and a perfect showcase for your talents and abilities.

If you have a superior demo reel, a good attitude, boundless creativity, phenomenal skills, and cheerful determination, you are well on your way to pursue a career that is fun, constantly evolving, and consistently satisfying.

You Are Here

The path to a career in visual effects begins with an obsession with visuals and the many possibilities of their creation.

Are you meticulous and do you have vast stores of patience? Even with computers, the work involved in creating excellent visual effects can take a phenomenally long time. An entire day's work can yield as little as five seconds of film. The best visual effects artists are the ones who are as in love with the process as the end result, and who can tune out everything else and focus on the tiniest details. As fun as the work can be, it is also arduous and you have to be someone who embraces that.

Are you creative and inventive, but also a good listener and team player? Artists must naturally have individual visions, but when you are working on a film, it is the director's vision to which you must adhere, and you must work with a large team to make it happen. That is not to say some of your own individuality will not come through, but you must be able to work as a team and keep the director's vision at the forefront of your daily duties.

Navigating the Terrain

Where are you now?

I am a skilled artist and computer graphics designer

I am taking design classes and am a computer whiz

I am good with computers but have no other art skills

Make your demo reel and volunteer for student films

Build a portfolio and create your own effects for a demo reel

Enroll in night, summer, or a one-year art and design course

Look for opportunities as an unpaid intern or PA in a visual effects department

Build up your computer skills and design effects for a demo reel

Organizing Your Expedition

Have everything in order before you set out.

Know some Hollywood history. While it may seem as though the world of visual effects is all about embracing the new, the best visual artists have a deep knowledge and love of what came before that informs their work. The hands-on approach and meticulous devotion that Ray Harryhausen undertook to produce characters in *Jason and the Argonauts* and *The Golden Voyage of Sinbad* inspires many visual effects specialists. History shows that simplicity can be the key to stunning visuals. The cyclone in *The Wizard of Oz* was created using a fan, a wire, and a woman's stocking, along with a brilliant use of light and a lot of trial and error. Seen on the big screen, the effect is still evocative and even terrifying. Visual effects artists are very proud of their history and their innovations.

Essential Gear

The latest software. Software is expensive, but it is the key to your potential livelihood. If the work you are interested in is all computer-based, you must pay attention to new software and find a way of acquiring it. You will be expected to know the names of every new innovation (such as the latest version of After Effects and Spine 3D), what they can do, and how they work.

Take more classes. While most of what you learn will be on the job, you can never go wrong taking more classes. If you are best with computers, you should definitely take some drawing classes, because the hands-on approach will help you better understand style and technique and improve your computer work. Courses can expose you to many different specialties within the field and help you find your niche. A well-rounded educational background will also look well on your résumé.

Volunteer to work on short and student projects. You learn best by doing, and while you should absolutely be experimenting with your own ideas, working on a film is the best way to understand how to do good work on a deadline, as part of a team, and in support of a director's vision. Any film project gives the opportunity to learn patience and develop a sense of humor.

Landmarks

If you are in your twenties... You should be spending every free minute working on projects for your demo reel. You should be taking classes in sculpture and design and reading up on the history of the art of visual effects. If you are not in a formal course program, volunteer for as many student or short films as you can manage while determining your specialty.

Stories from the Field
Angela Barson
Visual effects supervisor
London, England

Barson is one of the busiest visual effects supervisors in the industry, with such credits as the new *Casino Royale* (some of the striking visuals in the opening title card sequence are her work), *Curse of the Golden Flower*, and *Sweeney Todd* to her name. She began her career working at Parallax/Avid in 1994 where she developed software for paint and compositing packages. She then transitioned into digital composition herself, working on *Lara Croft: Tomb Raider* and several other films and television, including the first three *Harry Potter* films. Her talent and extreme dedication helped her advance quickly, producing visual effects for period, fantasy, and contemporary films.

Barson works for Moving Picture Co. (MPC) in London and continues to be closely involved with the development of compositing technology and is a mentor to junior staff.

In talking about her work on *Curse of the Golden Flower*, Barson explained that the challenge is to make the digital crowds look real through compositing. The goal of the live action film is to be as perfect as possible, but when creating CG, the compositor tries to put in glitches and imperfections to more closely simulate reality.

If you are in your thirties or forties... Pick your desired specialty as quickly as you can, carefully prepare your demo reel, then research people working in that field and ask for informational interviews. Whomever you meet with will most likely be happy to look at your demo reel and offer more targeted advice and perhaps be able to forward your résumé to some contacts.

If you are in your fifties... If you know where you want to specialize, look for targeted classes that may be taught by veterans in the field. They will probably be in your age range and will be open to talking with and

For Barson's work to continue to be effective, she keeps up to date with all new technologies and compositing programs. A particularly difficult shot for a film required a documentary-style look that was not going to work with any of the then-usual methods, so she quickly adopted an emerging technology, which ultimately saved the shot, and weeks of work.

Even an effect as old and basic as erasing safety wires on performers in a film can be improved. For a Hong Kong action movie, removing wires can be far more difficult than on average action films, simply because the action moves so much faster. Barson was quick to adapt another new technology for this kind of painstaking work.

A talented, successful, and respected visual effects artist like Barson knows that to continue working at the top of the game, she must take on a variety of projects, like modern comedies, period dramas, and action pictures, to keep all her skills fresh and focused. She must also constantly adapt to new formats and software programs, as well as work with developers to create innovative programs that will further enhance visual effects. Sometimes, she will simply have to go over something again and again for hours, days, or weeks, just to get it right. And that takes teamwork, trust, patience, and humor.

advising you and gearing you toward likely possibilities. If you have had a background in computers and visual arts, you may find it easier to transition into this career.

If you are over sixty... Do not be put off by the common stereotype that it is a young person's game. Visual effects do not require the physical stamina of many other professions in film and television; it requires intelligence, creativity, patience, skill, and endless attention to detail. A good demo reel will get attention no matter your age and if you have the right attitude and seem pleasant to work with, you will find yourself welcomed into the fold.

Further Resources

The Visual Effects Society The only organization representing the full breadth of visual effects artists, it notes events, offers a newsletter, job board, and list of members. http://www.visualeffectssociety.com

Industrial Light and Magic (ILM) The granddaddy of visual effects studios, founded by George Lucas, the Web site has features, news, employment possibilities, and a list of employees, which is useful for candidates who are preparing for informational interviews. http://www.ilm.com

Set Decorator/Art Department Coordinator

Set Decorator/Art Department Coordinator

Career Compasses

Guide yourself into the art department.

Relevant Knowledge of drawing, drafting, history, the structure of film and the way a space will look on film (40%)

Organizational Skills to manage sketches, research materials, and many different members of a team working on a variety of projects (25%)

Communication Skills to work well with your own team, that of the other departments, the director, and the production staff (25%)

Caring about doing detailed, quality work that services the story (10%)

Destination: Set Decorator/Art Department Coordinator

Even in this era of CGI, a lot of hands-on work is still done in the art department. In brief, the art department creates every interior seen in a film. It will also either create or decorate the exterior. The set decoration department dresses, or decorates, every set. Anything you see that creates a room, such as furniture, pictures, shelves, books, filing cabinets, etc. is all arranged and placed by the set decorators.

It is important to note that set decoration does not include props. Anything that is handled by an actor is a prop and therefore handled by the prop department, which works far more closely with the director. While children's artwork on a refrigerator is often the domain of the art and set decoration departments, if it is going to be filmed in close-up or discussed in some way, it becomes a prop. Anything else that creates the visual look of the film is the domain of the art department.

It may seem as though the art departments on period and fantasy films have more work to do than those on contemporary films. If you look at the nominees for art Oscars over the decades, you will see that the bulk are for period and fantasy films. However, creating a realistic, effective space in a modern film requires a lot of detail work that may go underappreciated. Jane Ann Stewart, production designer on the Oscar-winning film *Sideways*, spoke of the little details that went into shaping the look of the characters' everday worlds, like the warm messiness of the apartments that denoted the fullness and yet complexity of their lives. Unexpected details add depth to the film and give the actors more to work with. Specifically, Stewart situated the apartments of the two main characters on the second floor of their buildings. This was to suggest, however obliquely, that, although the men had a lot of growing up to do, the two were essentially on the same level. This is the kind of creative thinking that enhances a film and gets a production designer regular work.

The art and set decoration departments employ a variety of professionals, from buyers and coordinators to construction workers and painters, to illustrators, assistant art directors, art directors and the set decorators. Coordinating can be a bit more like office management than art, but the role is essential, pays well, and allows you to work on several different projects. No matter what the role, everyone who works in the art department does so because they have a passion for art and film and want to contribute their specific skill to making the completed project a special work of art.

Art departments always need unpaid interns, and 99 percent of the time, this will be someone's first job. An intern who does well, has a good attitude, and is friendly and personable will usually be able to land a low-paying job as a production assistant (PA) on another film. Again, if a person proves him- or herself as a PA, he or she may advance to a position as a coordinator on their next job. This is an important step, because you can join the union and begin to accrue benefits. (These benefits include the all-important unemployment insurance, which is a great help during the inevitable periods between jobs, which can sometimes last months.) For nearly all jobs, the art director will still want to hire someone he or she either knows, or who is highly recommended by someone they like and respect. As with almost every job in film and television, art department work is gained via word of mouth, which is why doing good work and being easy to get along with is so vital to success.

Essential Gear

A digital camera. The art and set decoration departments can often supply you with these, but you will look more professional if you have your own. For someone who wants to work their way up in set decorating, you should be taking pictures of anything that strikes you when you are visiting prop houses and cataloging it on your own computer. Years later, someone might be looking for a particular kind of clock, and if you took a picture of something like that and know where to find it, you will be noted as someone good to keep hiring.

Coordinating requires extensive organizational skills. It can be very similar to being an executive assistant in a busy office. There are a lot of strict deadlines and difficult temperaments to contend with. The entire production staff begins work when a project is in preproduction. On the first day of a new job, a coordinator may find he or she has to set up the art office, including ordering furniture, phones, and art supplies. During the time of preproduction, the staff will work comparatively short hours, usually about 10 hours per day. Once filming begins, the days stretch to around 12 hours and a coordinator must work with everyone in the art department to make sure that all is on track and that everyone has what they need. The coordinators in the art and set decoration departments usually liaise with each other regularly.

For the coordinator who wants to move into art direction, a portfolio of artwork opens doors. A coordinator whom people know is interested in moving up may sometimes be asked to design some small item for a film, or do more involved research. Although this work may not be credited, it can help you get a promotion. A set decoration coordinator who wants to move up must have a passion for interior design and develop a photographic memory for props and pieces.

While very few people who get into the art department end up as production designers, the work can still be exciting, creative, and lucrative for someone who loves visuals and is devoted to the craft.

You Are Here

The path to a job in the art department begins with an interest in visuals and love of film.

Do you have a good eye, some knowledge of art, and a general understanding of design? Production designers put together a team that is in love with visuals, and everyone is expected to at least have some basic knowledge of what comprises good art and design. The ability to speak the language of art and design is key to getting even an unpaid internship in an art department.

Do you have excellent organizational skills? You may work as a coordinator for several years before getting a chance to move up, and organizational skills are absolutely vital to the job. For a period or fantasy film, the art department may have a huge library of reference books, which you have to keep track of and in order. Art departments maintain files of paint and fabric swatches, sketches, photographs, and other art-related items. A coordinator also often tackles simple repair jobs around the office. If a coffee machine or photocopier breaks, you may be responsible for arranging a replacement or repair. If the creative team calls in while on location and you are in the office, you jump to handle their requests. A successful on-set artist not only brings design and aesthetic talent to a job, but practical skills that make sure a department runs efficiently.

Are you easygoing and able to keep your ego in check? An art director may hire an assistant solely based on excellent drafting skills, but that person must still contribute as a team player to advance. Furthermore, you cannot get possessive about your work. Sometimes a piece you poured your heart into ends up discarded. You simply have to accept it and move on.

Navigating the Terrain

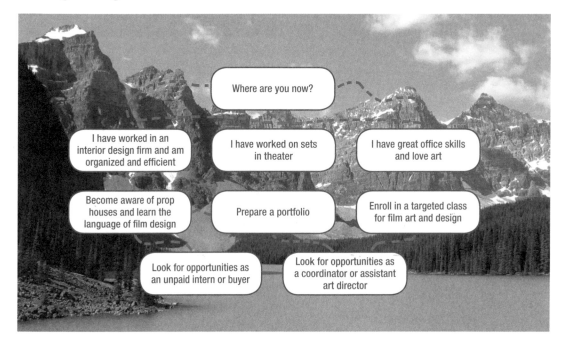

Where are you now?

I have worked in an interior design firm and am organized and efficient

I have worked on sets in theater

I have great office skills and love art

Become aware of prop houses and learn the language of film design

Prepare a portfolio

Enroll in a targeted class for film art and design

Look for opportunities as an unpaid intern or buyer

Look for opportunities as a coordinator or assistant art director

Organizing Your Expedition

Have your kit ready before you begin to travel.

Situate yourself in either Los Angeles or New York. The bulk of the work in the film and television industries is in these two cities, especially if you are interested in art. However, opportunities may spring up in other major cities such as Atlanta, Houston, Chicago, Seattle, and San Francisco.

Take some technical art classes. You may have a degree in fine art and be very good at drawing, but anyone aspiring to do artwork in an art department must master the basics in architecture and drafting. You must understand proportion, contour, and mass. Specific skills are necessary to design sets via computer graphics. Your portfolio is not ready to show an art director until it has several good samples of drafting.

Prepare your portfolio. In addition to the all-important drafting, your portfolio should show the extent of your skills and creativity. You should have examples of different kinds of movie sets or design elements so that employers know the range of your capabilities. Although your interest may lie solely in period or fantasy films, opportunities come up in all genres, so diversity matters. Do not limit yourself to castles and monsters. Present drawings of modern kitchens, schoolrooms, and street scenes. As an unpaid intern or production assistant, ask the art team for a portfolio critique and find out what they think. They may even show you their own portfolios, which can give you ideas on how to improve your own.

Essential Gear

Portfolio. Most workers in art departments begin at the very bottom in an unpaid position and it may be several jobs before you are asked to draw something. Still, you should be able to show off what you can do through a diverse portfolio. This is how you get taken seriously and advance in the field.

Volunteer to work on short, student, documentary, and independent features. For coordinators and assistants looking to move up, take advantage of downtime. Hone your skills by doing art direction and production design on small projects for free. On projects like these, you will often be the sole member of the design team, and your skills at coordinating will be invaluable as you balance the challenges of design on a budget. The project may later be entered in festivals and competitions, or even receive a small commercial release. That exposure can rocket your career to a higher level.

Arrange informational interviews. In Hollywood, as in many other businesses, it is all about who you know. Even an unpaid internship may require a recommendation. If you have few or zero contacts in the industry, try your university's alumni association. Chances are, someone who went to your school is now working in the industry in some capacity. The connection to your college can be enough for a fellow alum to at least take a look at your résumé, set up an informational interview, and maybe even connect you to an internship or first job.

Notes from the Field
Diana Goodwin
Art department coordinator/art director
Los Angeles, California

What were you doing before you decided to change careers?

I'd been to graduate school for medieval art history and museum studies and then worked in an interior design studio, but wasn't really satisfied. I took a job as content editor for a technology publisher's Web portal, which meant I could work from home. This was really helpful, because when I decided to move to L.A, I could take my day job with me.

Why did you change your career?

I found the academic environment to be too slow and conservative. I wanted to do work that involved more creativity at a faster pace. I've always loved movies and been fascinated with the design element, especially in fantasy films. So I decided to move to L.A. and get into an art department where I could use my artistic skills and knowledge and be more hands-on.

How did you make the transition?

Once I was settled in L.A, I decided to take an art directing class at UCLA Extension. It had been a long time since I'd done art and I wanted to get back in practice and learn some of what's involved in doing art for film. I became friendly with a classmate who had some connections at Warner Brothers Studios. He passed my résumé along to his contact,

Landmarks

If you are in your twenties... This is a good time to take as many classes as you can so as to build up your portfolio while securing an unpaid internship.

If you are in your thirties or forties... If you do not have drafting skills, you can still look for unpaid internships or even jobs as a PA while taking classes. If you have an artistic background and have worked in a team capacity, you will be a desirable candidate for the art and set decoration departments.

who passed it to the art department that was being set up for the film *Rock Star* and needed some unpaid interns. I was offered the position and when the film was over, someone I'd worked with helped me get a job as a set department coordinator for the film *Evolution*. I've since worked as an art department coordinator on several films, including *Ocean's Twelve*, and was an art director on the nature documentary *Sea Monsters: A Prehistoric Adventure*.

What are the keys to success in your new career?

"Just say yes." Anything someone asks you to do, say "yes" and find the way to get it done. You get work via word of mouth, so your interpersonal skills are one of the most important aspects of doing well. You have to be competent, pleasant, helpful, and nice to be around. A sense of humor is crucial, especially when you're working 12-hour days. You have to contribute, anticipate, and figure out what's needed without being asked. People are usually nice, but they don't want to have to stop and explain things, they want someone who is a step ahead and knows how to make their lives easier and the department run more smoothly. You learn everything on the job and the more you pick up on the job, the better you'll do then, and the more likely someone will hire you or recommend you for another job. You should also take any opportunity to stretch within the job and take on a bit more responsibility. You have to be resourceful, quick, and organized. And you have to network. Most of the jobs you get will be because of who you know, so you really want to develop a reputation as a good team player.

If you are in your fifties... Ift the bulk of your work experience has been in an office environment, especially doing office management or something similar, and you have artistic knowledge and some capacity, you are an ideal coordinator, provided you also have boundless energy and are able and willing to work long hours. If you have drafting skills or have worked in an interior design firm in a hands-on capacity, you may be able to bypass coordinating and be eligible for a higher position.

If you are over sixty... You may do better approaching the art departments in television, rather than film, as television can be somewhat more welcoming and tends to be less arduous and unpredictable. However, strong artistic knowledge and skills, as well as the ability to work well on a team, will be valued in any area and can still secure you a coordinating position.

Further Resources

The School of the Art Institute of Chicago If you want to pursue formal education in art preparatory to a job in film, this is one of the best schools in the country. http://www.saic.edu

Set Decorators Society of America A very useful Web site dedicated to the craft of set decoration. There are links for resources, a magazine, articles, events, a members directory, and contact info. http://www.setdecorators.org

Art Directors Guild Features links to magazines, publications, events, and further resources. http://www.artdirectors.org

Wardrobe Department Worker

Wardrobe Department Worker

Career Compasses

Guide yourself into the world of costume.

Relevant Knowledge of costume, styles, sewing, and fabrics (25%)

Organizational Skills for managing all the clothes and accessories, as well as sketches, swatches, photos, and tools for an entire production, often in a very small space (30%)

Communication Skills to not only work well within the wardrobe department where things might change constantly and everyone must be up to speed, but also to work well with performers and every other department on the production (25%)

Ability to Manage Stress in a high-paced environment where the work is hard and the hours are long (20%)

Destination: Wardrobe Department Worker

Certainly, an audience can admire beautiful, well-fitting clothes that define each character, but the clothes should be so well integrated so as to be an inherent part of the the film or television production. Legendary costume designer Edith Head, winner of eight Academy Awards, said that a costume should support, not compete with, story and character development. She saw how clothes could be more than dressing—they could be part of the story. The famous dress worn by Bette Davis in *All*

About Eve shows a woman wedded to glamour, desperate to demonstrate her sexiness compared to that of a much younger woman. Head's period costumes for the classic comedy *The Court Jester* are not traditionally medieval—cuts and colors are used to heighten the comedy. The wardrobe department always assures that each character looks his or her best and exactly right.

The wardrobe department offers many jobs, including costume designer, costume supervisor, wardrobe supervisor, and wardrobe assistant. A good wardrobe supervisor runs a very tight ship. Because problems always come up on film and television sets, professional wardrobe workers learn how to solve them with maximum speed and minimal fuss. The entire wardrobe team must be able to think quickly and inventively and remain calm at all times.

Budding wardrobe assistants take entry-level positions assisting in the daily creation and maintenance of all the clothes in a movie or television show. Duties include fitting and dressing the actors, mending and altering costumes, packing and unpacking costumes and accessories, cleaning and ironing, helping to make pieces and put costumes together, making sure that everything is available when needed, keeping accurate records of what is needed, and storing costumes and returning anything that was rented.

Keeping accurate wardrobe records is very important for continuity in film and television. Scenes are shot out of sequence, and for a film, a particular "day" can be revisited weeks after a section of it was shot. Every performer must wear exactly what they wore the first time that day was shot, down to the smallest piece of jewelry. It is the assistant's job to keep track of every item and not lose or misplace a thing.

To become a wardrobe assistant, you do not need formal qualifications, although these can certainly help. Even if you are working on a television show set where all the clothes are bought, you still must have good hand and machine sewing skills and know how to cut patterns and build clothes.

Even on a long-running, well-oiled television series, the work environment in wardrobe can be very stressful. The hours are often long, with a day beginning at 5 A.M. to assure all the clothes needed are clean and ready, and not ending till well into the evening. For film, the initial prep work involving the building and fitting of costumes may only last a week or so, but everyone from the costume designer down to the assistants will be working almost round the clock. Once the shoot is underway, you will still be working at least 12-hour days. Whether in a studio or on a film location, the workrooms are nearly always small, cramped, and hot.

Everyone in wardrobe must have good people skills. Costume designers coordinate with the film's director on shaping a look for each character, and with the production designer to assure that the color schemes and patterns of the clothes will work with those of the sets. Efficient costume departments operate on delegation and diplomacy. If the performers come in for fittings and complain about designs or comfort, the wardrobe staff must remain calm and employ the tact necessary to work through these issues. A costumer may have to compromise his or her vision in order to please performers and directors. Flexibility is important, as is the ability to communicate well. If a piece must look a certain way in order to be historically accurate, a costumer should be able to explain this to a director and performer in a way that will be respected. It is important to build a reputation as a quality costumer who knows his or her stuff and who is pleasant to work with.

Essential Gear

Portfolio. It really cannot be emphasized enough that a portfolio is the way to show your capabilities. Even if you show up to volunteer, a portfolio makes you look serious and professional. It can just be a small sketchbook, or photographs of costumes made for kids, but people want to know you are creative and capable.

It is not only crucial to get along well with the entire wardrobe team and production staff, wardrobe experts must foster good relationships with colleagues throughout the business. Whether you are in film, television, or theater, the communities are small and everyone knows everyone. You never know when you will need to call in a favor. When Carey Bennett, the costumer on the television show *Scrubs*, was told at 5 P.M. one day to produce about a dozen outfits echoing the character "Rerun" from the 1970s sitcom *What's Happening!* for a scene the next morning, she had to call in favors to fabric-selling friends who had closed for the day. She rushed to get required sizes for each performer for the scene, and she called in extra people to assist with sewing all night. The scene lasts about 45 seconds, and all the costumes are perfect, an example of the sort of commitment and teamwork necessary for a quality costume department.

Because competition is fierce, you must create a portfolio or "reel" that truly advertises your skills. You can build this portfolio by taking on work in student theater and films, community theater, working as a "daily" (temp) on a film or television show, or working for a costume rental shop. If a costumer whose work you admire is about to start on a new film, you can call the production office and ask if they need any unpaid interns. If the costume supervisor agrees to meet with you, you will want your portfolio to make a favorable impression.

As with most jobs in the industry, wardrobe work is freelance. Even the most sought-after costume designers only work from film to film. Building a reputation as a great team player with abilities, ideas, and a good attitude will help you gain employment opportunities.

You Are Here

The journey into the world of costume often begins from a love of history and aesthetics.

Do you know a lot about historical clothing and current styles, or are you an avid researcher? Most costumers come to their work from a longtime interest in the look of the clothed body and the changes in costume over the centuries. Male and female costumers alike often speak of parents who sewed and taught their children to sew, or who were involved in fashion in some way. Regular trips to museums may have stoked their interest in historical fabrics and fashions. When costuming a period film or show, good design is about more than just re-creating exact styles. It is about tailoring fabrics and colors to suit performers, characters, and the overall look of the film. Sandy Powell, the Oscar-winning costumer for *Shakespeare in Love*, described the costume she created for Geoffrey Rush's character and explained to Rush that his character was a "one-suit man." Rush found this enormously useful in locating the behavior and mien of the character. You also have to have an eye for what flatters a body and a passion for research because creating period clothes can require months of historical study. Even wardrobe assistants, especially those who want to become designers, should have a thorough knowledge of the historical aspect of the clothes they are handling.

Do you draw well and can you sew and mend quickly under pressure? In a wardrobe department, even fussy work like beading must be done at top speed under a tight deadline. You also have to be prepared for disaster. If a costume rips on a piece of scenery, the wardrobe professional must fix it then and there.

Do you have a strong sense of how to dress someone in a flattering outfit from any historical period? There is more to good modern costuming than selecting clothes in an actor's correct size. An actor may have a long neck, a short waist, or unusually proportioned hips. An excellent costumer understands how to work with these characteristics so that the actor will look great. Colors, styles, and fabrics all have to be selected with both the look of the performer and the needs of the character in mind.

Navigating the Terrain

Where are you now?

I have taken some classes, and have top-notch sewing skills

I have been drawing and sewing as a hobby for years

I used to sew and draw a lot but have not in a while

Review and polish your portfolio

Enroll in a targeted class for costuming that discusses business as well as design

Visit a crafts store to rediscover your tastes and learn what's current

Seek out paid wardrobe positions

Resume practicing your craft; volunteer for regional theater productions

Organizing Your Expedition

Gather all the guides you can before heading out.

Prepare your portfolio. Even if you have no experience or credits, you should still have a portfolio of drawings and photos of your clothes to show prospective employers. A portfolio should demonstrate as much diversity as possible. Working on a student film or theatrical production can show that you can design on a budget.

Essential Gear

Sewing and sketching kit. If you have been hired as a wardrobe assistant for a multimillion dollar film, the wardrobe department should be well stocked. However, you should never enter any job expecting to be provided with the basic wardrobe tools. Wardrobe workers wear tape measures around their necks like doctors wear stethoscopes, and you should provide your own, as well as a wrist pin cushion, scissors, and seam ripper. You do not have to carry around a gigantic box filled with every possible sewing tool, but an aspiring wardrobe worker must have his or her own quality equipment at hand and should keep at least a small sketchbook and pencil handy as well. Even if you never end up using any of it, you will look more professional having it available.

Consider taking courses. Not all costume designers go to design school, but credentials from a respected institution can definitely be useful in securing work. Classes can hone sewing and design skills. Schools like the Fashion Institute of Design & Merchandising (FIDM), based in Los Angeles, or New York University's Tisch School of the Arts, have costume programs that will not only teach you basics, but fully ground you in costume history, as well as the business aspects of the industry. A degree from one of these schools may impress a prospective employer. By taking courses, you can make professional contacts, hear about jobs, and get involved in quality student productions.

Volunteer in a small theater. While the workings of wardrobe departments for film and television are very different from theater, being involved in a theatrical production is a good way to gain experience.

Stories from the Field

Patricia Field
Costume designer
New York, New York

Patricia Field is the winner of Emmy Awards and Costume Designers Guild Awards for her fashion-forward costuming on *Sex and the City*, and Oscar-nominated for her work on *The Devil Wears Prada*. Field was first a fashion designer with a Greenwich Village boutique in the 1960s. Although the fields are obviously related, being a fashion designer is a very different track from costume design. When you apply for design schools, you will find that they are two different programs and you are expected to choose one or the other. Patricia Field is the very rare fashion designer to make the transition from design to costuming.

One of the biggest differences between being a fashion designer and being a costume designer is teamwork. A fashion designer can listen to his or her own ideas and go with what feels right. A costumer must work with a director and performers, many of whom do not know clothes but still have strong ideas about what they want. While a fashion designer creates clothes for a style of man or woman, a costumer is presented with a group of characters with distinct personalities and must outfit each one to suit those personalities. For Field, a designer with an outsize personality and deep adoration for clothes and story telling, this came naturally.

A small clientele loved Field's boutique in New York, but she was otherwise unknown. She started to do some styling for a few small movies and television shows. When she was working on the 1995 film *Miami*

Landmarks

If you are in your twenties... This is a good time to apply for a place at a design school. If you need to work while in school, try to get a job in a costume shop, or anyplace where you will get to handle clothes and learn techniques of costume maintenance. The education and hands-on experience will make it much easier for you to get a job as a wardrobe assistant later.

Rhapsody, she met actress Sarah Jessica Parker. The two bonded instantly, and three years later, when *Sex and the City* was going into production, Parker asked that Field be brought in as the costumer. After 30 years of working in the fashion industry, Field quickly became a household name.

Although she was knowledgeable and experienced, the challenges of outfitting four very different women every week were still immense. A lot of thought and shopping and combing through selections went into every episode. A vast selection of shoes, jewelry, and other accessories had to be kept on hand at all times. Commenting on a particularly sensual scene where a character was shown slipping out of shoes, the executive producer explained that there were different shoes originally, but when Field saw what sort of mood was being created, she came back with very different shoes that heightened the romance of the scene. The characters also evolved throughout the series and the clothes had to keep pace. In season five, when two of the actresses were pregnant, outfits had to be carefully selected and worked with to hide the pregnancies.

Field's success as a costumer is in part due to her seeking inspiration in the actors. She paid close attention not just to the personality of Carrie Bradshaw, but the look and style of Parker. For *Prada*, she incorporated the striking qualities of Meryl Streep into the stylishness of Miranda Priestley. Field believes that to tell a story through clothes heightens the presence of the characters. She knows that clothes make the character, as well as the person, but that they also serve the story, rather than take center stage.

If you are in your thirties or forties... If you have not done any drawing or sewing in a while, you should take some classes and volunteer on a film or at a theater to get up to speed. If you have been sewing as a hobby and are good at handling high-pressure situations, whether in a paying career or shepherding a group of kids through a costumed performance, you can seek an unpaid internship on a film set or television show.

If you are in your fifties... If you have been sewing and cutting patterns for years but only as a hobby, volunteer for an independent film. Independent films try for a professional atmosphere and always need more people who are good at the work and do not need to be paid. If you do one job well and show you can handle it, people will be ready to trust you with another.

If you are over sixty... A wardrobe department will be especially interested if you have a unique sewing skill you learned as a kid that is not done so much anymore. Chances are, if you have been keeping up your abilities, you are just as handy with a needle as a twenty-something—and probably a lot more used to dealing with all sorts of people under fraught circumstances—so a wardrobe department will be very interested in bringing you on board.

Further Resources

Costume Designers Guild   Web site for the union representing costume designers, assistant costume designers and costume illustrators, it has a gallery and library and links to further resources. http://www.costumedesignersguild.com

The Costume Institute at the Metropolitan Museum of Art   Boasting one of the greatest costume collections in the world, the Museum unfortunately does not have a permanent exhibit, but regularly presents in-depth shows highlighting unique aspects of historical costume. The department can be approached for special research purposes. http://www.metmuseum.org

The Costumes Archive at Williams College   An online archive of dozens of costumes at a variety of angles. http://drm.williams.edu/costumes

Properties
Department Worker

Properties Department Worker

Career Compasses

Get a handle on where you are as a props person.

Relevant Knowledge of building, design, the structure and techniques of filmmaking, and the way props work well in a film (30%)

Caring about doing high-quality work at all times and maintaining a strong focus on detail, even after working a 12-hour day (25%)

Organizational Skills to keep track of hundreds of props and be sure that they are all in the exact condition necessary for the shoot at all times (25%)

Communication Skills to liaise well with everyone in the props department, as well as the art, wardrobe, and production crew, including the director (20%)

Destination: Properties Department Worker

Rosebud. The Maltese falcon. Wilson. These are famous film props that were not only integral aspects of the story, but almost characters in their own right. To be as wholly effective as they were and enhance the film in which they played a part, a strong, creative, and inventive properties team was required.

A prop is anything handled by an actor. There may be books in a case and lamps on a table, but if these are not touched or referred to by the characters, they are part of the set décor. If the lamp is picked up and used to beat another character to death, that is a prop. Many things must be considered in the choosing of the lamp. Is it to the owner's taste and something they could afford? Is it heavy enough to beat someone to death, even if the character doing the beating is not very strong? Is it light enough that the character can legitimately pick it up and wield it as a weapon long enough to kill someone? The prop itself is probably made of plastic, or something even lighter, but it must look the part.

The props department works closely with the director and the production designer to determine the look and style of every major prop used in the production. The property master oversees a large group of people whose job is to buy, acquire, or make all the necessary props. The prop master is also responsible for aspects of a prop's use in any given scene and works with the script supervisor to maintain continuity. There may be four versions of a teddy bear that gets increasingly worn through the script's story. Since scenes are shot out of order, different bears will be used on different days. It is the job of the props department to guarantee that the right bear is used for the right time in the story.

It may appear as though more work is involved in managing props for an action picture, a sumptuous period piece, or a medical drama on television, rather than a small independent film or a sitcom. Bear in mind that there will be larger properties departments for the larger projects, but that all productions will have a tremendous amount of props that have to be bought, made, or rented, and then recorded and looked after. From the pen a character uses to write down a crucial phone number to the car in which they make a daring escape, everything requires careful attention.

Someone who wants to work in a props department must be extremely well organized. A record must be made of every prop and each must be accounted for at all times when in use and then properly stored at the end of the day. When preparing for any shoot, the props department must keep lists of every prop needed for every character and note the progress of those props, whether they are being made, sent over from a rental company, or have been bought and are being shipped.

Additionally, a props worker must be detail-oriented. Many of the gilt and leather-bound books consulted by characters in the Harry Potter films will look very much alike. During a studying scene, the books will get picked up, handled, and rearranged. They may even get flown around a room and land in a pile. It is the job of the prop master to set them all back in the exact order they were in at the beginning of the scene each time the scene is to be reshot, no matter how many dozens of takes there are. Very likely, only the most eagle-eyed viewer watching a DVD would notice the mistake, but a prop master who cares about the quality of his other work will guarantee that such a mistake not occur.

Essential Gear

Résumé and list of abilities. As with most jobs in the industry, you get work via good word of mouth and contacts. Someone may know of a props department that is hiring and ask you to give them a résumé to send over. While you may not have film or theater credits, any work you have done that shows a need for organization and attention to detail is useful. You should also list all your abilities in terms of construction, craft, and design.

Your organization and attention to detail must remain sharp even after a long day. The props department often works longer than everyone else, because they have to be on the set early to see that everything is ready and working, and when the shoot has wrapped for the day, every prop must be accounted for, checked in, cleaned, and stored. This can take another two hours.

While you do not have to be a skilled artisan, it does not hurt. Anyone who wants to work with props should have some basic construction ability or an understanding of how things are built and how they work. Props will often break on set and anyone who works in the props department should be able to fix them. If a scene calls for a major fight, the props department will build breakaway furniture. (This is an item like a wooden chair that falls to pieces after being thrown against a wall or at a person.) The more construction skills you have, whether building furniture, ancient instruments, or pretty books and owl cages, the more in demand you will be.

An aspiring props worker must be a quick thinker. Even under the most planned and controlled conditions, something can go wrong and you have to be able to suggest a solution. Perhaps a prop was built for a specific actress to handle, but she was replaced at the last minute by an actress with smaller hands. If there is no time to replace the prop, can an unseen handle or grip be created? Is there a mesh glove the actress can wear that will not be captured on film? Is there even a different way she could hold the prop? The demands of a tight schedule and budget will not allow for slow consideration—the director will look to the props department to make it work.

The ability to remain calm is also paramount. If a prop breaks and the director is having a fit because the production is two days behind schedule, you may have to hammer the piece back together right there on the set. The person who can wield a hammer to perfection under such circumstances without breaking anything will go far.

As with most other professions in the industry, aspiring props workers must begin as either unpaid interns or production assistants in the props department and slowly work their way up, learning on the job. A love of building, creation, and film is necessary. Work in the props department can be very difficult, but with the right attitude, it can also be a lot of fun, so that every day feels like you are a little kid again, playing with toys.

You Are Here

The journey to a career in props begins with an interest in building and a love of styling things.

Are you obsessed with details in things and do you love research?
In film and television, the goods are in the details. You have to be the sort of person who cares that the ink and writing look exactly right for a hand-written "For Sale" sign in a turn-of-the-century French hat shop. You may spend hours researching such details, long before you sit down to create the sign. If you know that a character would only use a particular kind of candle to light his or her way down a rickety stairway, you must stop at nothing to find that candle and enjoy the thorough search. You do not have to be a historian, but you should embrace research and want to do as much as necessary to make sure that everything you give an actor to use suits that character.

Do you enjoy building things and can you do so in a timely manner?
Not everyone who works in props builds, and on big, complicated films, there will be many different departments where things are created. All the weaponry used in the Oscar-winning film *Gladiator* had to be built, meaning dozens and dozens of swords and axes. If the idea of such work is appealing to you, your abilities must not only be up to scratch, but you must be able to build everything assigned within the allotted time frame.

Are you good at compromising and a creative thinker? A director making a film set in the 1920s may want a character to use an item that was not invented until the 1950s, which you know after careful research. Most directors will yield to your better knowledge, but if they are stuck on the look of something, you have to be someone who can discuss it tactfully,

Navigating the Terrain

Where are you now?

I have worked with props in theater and on small films

I am detail-oriented and enjoy research

I am well organized and a skilled craftsperson

Prepare a portfolio and résumé

Take some classes in construction and craft

Volunteer to do props for a no-budget project

Look for opportunities as a props department PA

Build your network as you strengthen your skills

Organizing Your Expedition

Be ready for anything as you journey into the props department.

Get a gun license. Whether it is a Pirates of the Caribbean movie or one of the James Bond franchise, or even just a small independent film wherein one of the characters uses a gun, a lot of guns show up in films and, although the actors are shooting blanks, these guns are real. It is the job of the prop master to buy or rent and then maintain them, and the prop master must be legally qualified to handle guns. Almost wherever you are in the props department, knowing the basics of gun maintenance can be helpful. Guns will frequently jam and you want to be the person who can step up and fix them.

Take a series of crafts classes. The props department is one area where being a jack-of-all-trades is incredibly useful, both to the project and to your career arc. If a very detailed and accurate ancient lute is needed, a specialized artisan will be hired, but the more basic skills you have, the better. When a character in a film is knitting a baby blanket, someone in the props department (or perhaps even wardrobe or art) probably knitted it and set up the needles for the character to use. Male or female, you want to be the one who can raise your hand and volunteer to create that prop. You also want to be able to build a tree house or a detonator. Or, if you are out shopping for the exact floor lamp for a middle-class home in the 1910s and find a broken one in a second-hand shop, you want to be able to rewire it and make it look new. The bulk of work in props will involve shopping for modern items and keeping track of them during a shoot, but the more you know how to do, the more people will want to use you and the further and faster your career will accelerate.

Essential Gear

A good tool kit. If you are taking a job where you know there will be a lot of on-set construction, you must show up for work the first day with your own tools. On a no-budget film, there will not be any tools, and on a big-budget production, you cannot expect that the tool chest is open to everyone. The property master may tell you to go put your kit back in the car, that they have specialized equipment on hand for you to use, but you will look more serious and professional if you do not expect anyone to lend you a hammer.

Learn the basics in graphics and filmmaking. The props department works closely with the art department in shaping the look of every interior and exterior in a film. It is useful for someone who wants to work their way up in the props department to have at least a general sense of what is involved in decorating, like color, style, and texture. On a television show like *Sex and the City*—where look and design was so specific and played such an important role in the show—the props department worked with the art and wardrobe departments in choosing certain props, but also worked inventively and paid close attention to all aspects of contemporary design to give every character the right props. At least a simple understanding of filmmaking techniques is also useful. Knowing

Stories from the Field
Ty Teiger
Property master
Los Angeles, California

Ty Teiger has been lucky to have the sort of career that most aspiring prop masters probably dream of, working on such films as *Star Wars: The Phantom Menace*, *Star Wars: Attack of the Clones* and the James Bond film *Casino Royale*. He freely admits, however, that despite a long, varied, and distinguished set of credits like his, the chance to work on such films is pretty rare.

Working on fantasy films is a particular challenge, because the prop designs must come solely from your imagination. In a contemporary piece, you can buy or rent props. For a period piece, you research the correct items and either build, buy, or rent them. It can take more work, but you have a basis from which to work. On a film like *Star Wars: The Phantom Menace*, however, the props must be unique and look like they are exactly what you would find a long time ago in a galaxy far, far away. Not only does the work require immense thought and imagination, it is also time-consuming and laborious, with some 2,500 props required per film, and close to 80 percent hand-built or created using random items such as bubble bath bottles and Christmas tree stands.

how a shot is framed will help you choose the best props for a given shot. On the job, you will soon learn what looks good and what does not. A sword that is beautiful in the rental shop may be better suited for theater than film. The more you pay attention to the structure and technique of film, the better you will be at choosing props.

Landmarks

If you are in your twenties... Concentrate on building up your skills. Volunteer to work on small films and plays. This is a good time to take a lot of unpaid work and just focus on mastering the basics and making contacts.

Teiger began his career as a dressing prop person on a small film, then worked on obscure television shows as a prop master for a number of years, eventually transitioning back into film. He embraces the variety of the work, having worked on period films such as *Richard III* and *The English Patient* as well as the big-budget extravaganzas.

Teiger's job is to oversee everything that goes into the world of props on a show. He also supervises the action hand props. When a script is broken down in preproduction, he can see which props will be needed and work from descriptions to begin initial designs. The initial focus is on hand props for the actors, because these are the hardest and will be noticed the most. Once those are in place, work begins on smaller background pieces.

The advent of hi-definition film has meant that Teiger and his crew must focus even more closely on detail and intricacy. A digital camera means everything is always in focus, so there is no opportunity to slack off or cut corners, because lesser work will be seen.

In considering the importance of good props, Teiger notes that they give a show more reality. Without props, actors would give lines, but they would not really be doing anything. Inasmuch as people in real life are constantly handling objects, so must people in film, and those objects must look true to the character and the world, whether it is today's world, that of several hundred years ago, or one that never was.

If you are in your thirties or forties... If you already have good building and crafts skills and are working in an environment that demands organization and attention to detail, you can probably try for a job as a set PA. Build up some credits first by working on smaller films, for which you will probably have to volunteer.

If you are in your fifties... If you have a number of excellent skills and a really strong understanding about how props work—perhaps you have been involved in community theater—you may be able to try for a job as a low-paid PA first, rather than take unpaid work. If you are willing to take unpaid work, however, that may be a way to begin building a good reputation.

If you are over sixty... If you already have a gun license and a number of skills, as well as one or two highly specialized skills in building or crafts, you may be in a good position to apply for jobs in television or commercials. The pace is still fast, but there will be more of a general acceptance of someone who has the ability but is coming into the industry a bit later.

Further Resources

Independent Feature Project Among other things, the IFP will list jobs and note features going into production. An independent feature is a great place to ask for free work and start to gain invaluable experience. http://www.ifp.org

Women In Film Not only does the site have a message board and lists of jobs both paid and unpaid, but new members can ask for mentors in their chosen field. A mentor can not only advise you, but sometimes put you in contact with someone who needs an extra hand on set. http://www.wif.org

Appendix A

Going Solo: Starting Your Own Business

Starting your own business can be very rewarding—not only in terms of potential financial success, but also in the pleasure derived from building something from the ground up, contributing to the community, being your own boss, and feeling reasonably in control of your fate. However, business ownership carries its own obligations—both in terms of long hours of hard work and new financial and legal responsibilities. If you succeed in growing your business, your responsibilities only increase. Many new business owners come in expecting freedom only to find themselves chained tighter to their desks than ever before. Still, many business owners find greater satisfaction in their career paths than do workers employed by others.

The Internet has also changed the playing field for small business owners, making it easier than ever before to strike out on your own. While small mom-and-pop businesses such as hairdressers and grocery stores have always been part of the economic landscape, the Internet has made reaching and marketing to a niche easier and more profitable. This has made possible a boom in *microbusinesses*. Generally, a microbusiness is considered to have under ten employees. A microbusiness is also sometimes called a *SoHo* for "small office/home office."

The following appendix is intended to explain, in general terms, the steps in launching a small business, no matter whether it is selling your Web-design services or opening a pizzeria with business partners. It will also point out some of the things you will need to bear in mind. Remember also that the particular obligations of your municipality, state, province, or country may vary, and that this is by no means a substitute for doing your own legwork. Further suggested reading is listed at the end.

Crafting a Business Plan

It has often been said that success is 1 percent inspiration and 99 percent perspiration. However, the interface between the two can often be hard to achieve. The first step to taking your idea and making it reality is constructing a viable *business plan*. The purpose of a business plan is to think things all the way through, to make sure your ideas really are profitable, and to figure out the "who, what, when, where, why, and how" of your business. It fills in the details for three areas: your goals, why you think they are attainable, and how you plan to get to there. "You need to know where you're going before you take that first step," says Drew Curtis, successful Internet entrepreneur and founder of the popular newsfilter Fark.com.

Take care in writing your business plan. Generally, these documents contain several parts: An *executive summary* stating the essence of the plan; a *market summary* explaining how a need exists for the product and service you will supply and giving an idea of potential profitability by comparing your business to similar organizations; a *company description* which includes your products and services, why you think your organization will succeed, and any special advantages you have, as well as a description of *organization* and *management*; and your *marketing and sales strategy*. This last item should include market highlights and demographic information and trends that relate to your proposal. Also include a *funding request* for the amount of start-up capital you will need. This is supported by a section on *financials*, or the sort of cash flow you can expect, based on market analysis, projection, and comparison with existing companies. Other needed information, such as personal financial history, résumés, legal documents, or pictures of your product, can be placed in *appendices*.

Use your business plan to get an idea of how much startup money is necessary and to discipline your thinking and challenge your preconceived notions before you develop your cash flow. The business plan will tell you how long it will take before you turn a profit, which in turn is linked to how long it will before you will be able to pay back investors or a bank loan—which is something that anyone supplying you with money will want to know. Even if you are planning to subside on grants or you are not planning on investment or even starting a for-profit company, the discipline imposed by the business plan is still the first step to organizing your venture.

A business plan also gives you a realistic view of your personal financial obligations. How long can you afford to live without regular income? How are you going to afford medical insurance? When will your business begin turning a profit? How much of a profit? Will you need to reinvest your profits in the business, or can you begin living off of them? Proper planning is key to success in any venture.

A final note on business plans: Take into account realistic expected profit minus realistic costs. Many small business owners begin by underestimating start-ups and variable costs (such as electricity bills), and then underpricing their product. This effectively paints them into a corner from which it is hard to make a profit. Allow for realistic market conditions on both the supply and the demand side.

Partnering Up

You should think long and hard about the decision to go into business with a partner (or partners). Whereas other people can bring needed capital, expertise, and labor to a business, they can also be liabilities. The questions you need to ask yourself are:

☞ Will this person be a full and equal partner? In other words, are they able to carry their own weight? Make a full and fair assessment of your potential partner's personality. Going into business with someone who lacks a work ethic, or prefers giving directions to working in the trenches, can be a frustrating experience.

☞ What will they contribute to the business? For instance, a partner may bring in start-up money, facilities, or equipment. However, consider if this is enough of a reason to bring them on board. You may be able to get the same advantages in another way—for instance, renting a garage rather than working out of your partner's. Likewise, doubling skill sets does not always double productivity.

☞ Do they have any liabilities? For instance, if your prospective partner has declared bankruptcy in the past, this can hurt your collective venture's ability to get credit.

☞ Will the profits be able to sustain all the partners? Many start-up ventures do not turn profits immediately, and what little they do produce can be spread thin amongst many partners. Carefully work out the math.

Also bear in mind that going into business together can put a strain on even the best personal relationships. No matter whether it is family, friends, or strangers, keep everything very professional with written agreements regarding these investments. Get everything in writing, and be clear where obligations begin and end. "It's important to go into business with the right people," says Curtis. "If you don't—if it degrades into infighting and petty bickering—it can really go south quickly."

Incorporating. . . or Not

Think long and hard about incorporating. Starting a business often requires a fairly large—and risky—financial investment, which in turn exposes you to personal liability. Furthermore, as your business grows, so does your risk. Incorporating can help you shield yourself from this liability. However, it also has disadvantages.

To begin with, incorporating is not necessary for conducting professional transactions such as obtaining bank accounts and credit. You can do this as a sole proprietor, partnership, or simply by filing a DBA ("doing business as") statement with your local court (also known as "trading as" or an "assumed business name"). The DBA is an accounting entity that facilitates commerce and keeps your business' money separate from your own. However, the DBA does not shield you from responsibility if your business fails. It is entirely possible to ruin your credit, lose your house, and have your other assets seized in the unfortunate event of bankruptcy.

The purpose of incorporating is to shield yourself from personal financial liability. In case the worst happens, only the business' assets can be taken. However, this is not always the best solution. Check your local laws: Many states have laws that prevent a creditor from seizing a non-incorporated small business' assets in case of owner bankruptcy. If you are a corporation, however, the things you use to do business that are owned by the corporation—your office equipment, computers, restaurant refrigerators, and other essential equipment—may be seized by creditors, leaving you no way to work yourself out of debt. This is why it is imperative to consult with a lawyer.

There are other areas in which being a corporation can be an advantage, such as business insurance. Depending on your business needs, insurance can be for a variety of things: malpractice, against delivery failures or spoilage, or liability against defective products or accidents. Furthermore, it is easier to hire employees, obtain credit, and buy health insurance as an organization than as an individual. However, on the downside, corporations are subject to specific and strict laws concerning management and ownership. Again, you should consult with a knowledgeable legal expert.

Among the things you should discuss with your legal expert are the advantages and disadvantages of incorporating in your jurisdiction and which type of incorporation is best for you. The laws on liability and how much of your profit will be taken away in taxes vary widely by state and country. Generally, most small businesses owners opt for *limited liability companies* (LLCs), which gives them more control and a more flexible management structure. (Another possibility is a *limited liability partnership*, or *LLP*, which is especially useful for professionals such as doctors and lawyers.) Finally, there is the *corporation*, which is characterized by transferable ownerships shares, perpetual succession, and, of course, limited liability.

Most small businesses are sole proprietorships, partnerships, or privately-owned corporations. In the past, not many incorporated, since it was necessary to have multiple owners to start a corporation. However, this is changing, since it is now possible in many states for an individual to form a corporation. Note also that the form your business takes is usually not set in stone: A sole proprietorship or partnership can switch to become an LLC as it grows and the risks increase; furthermore, a successful LLC can raise capital by changing its structure to become a corporation and selling stock.

Legal Issues

Many other legal issues besides incorporating (or not) need to be addressed before you start your business. It is impossible to speak directly to every possible business need in this brief appendix, since regulations, licenses, and health and safety codes vary by industry and locality. A restaurant in Manhattan, for instance, has to deal not only with the usual issues such as health inspectors, the state liquor board, but obscure regulations such as New York City's cabaret laws, which prohibit dancing without a license in a place where alcohol is sold. An asbestos-abatement company, on the other hand, has a very different set of standards it has to abide by, including federal regulations. Researching applicable laws is part of starting up any business.

Part of being a wise business owner is knowing when you need help. There is software available for things like bookkeeping, business plans, and Web site creation, but generally, consulting with a knowledgeable professional—an accountant or a lawyer (or both)—is the smartest move. One of the most common mistakes is believing that just because you have expertise in the technical aspects of a certain field, you know all about running a business in that field. Whereas some people may balk at the expense, by suggesting the best way to deal with possible problems, as well as cutting through red tape and seeing possible pitfalls that you may not even have been aware of, such professionals usually more than make up for their cost. After all, they have far more experience at this than does a first-time business owner!

Financial

Another necessary first step in starting a business is obtaining a bank account. However, having the account is not as important as what you do with it. One of the most common problems with small businesses is undercapitalization—especially in brick-and-mortar businesses that sell or make something, rather than service-based businesses. The rule of thumb is that you should have access to money equal to your first year's anticipated profits, plus start-up expenses. (Note that this is not the same as having the money on hand—see the discussion on lines of credit, below.) For instance, if your annual rent, salaries, and equipment will cost $50,000 and you expect $25,000 worth of profit in your first year, you should have access to $75,000 worth of financing.

You need to decide what sort of financing you will need. Small business loans have both advantages and disadvantages. They can provide critical start-up credit, but in order to obtain one, your personal credit will need to be good, and you will, of course, have to pay them off with interest. In general, the more you and your partners put into the business yourselves, the more credit lenders will be willing to extend to you.

Equity can come from your own personal investment, either in cash or an equity loan on your home. You may also want to consider bringing on partners—at least limited financial partners—as a way to cover start-up costs.

It is also worth considering obtaining a line of credit instead of a loan. A loan is taken out all at once, but with a line of credit, you draw on the money as you need it. This both saves you interest payments and means that you have the money you need when you need it. Taking out too large of a loan can be worse than having no money at all! It just sits there collecting interest—or, worse, is spent on something utterly unnecessary—and then is not around when you need it most.

The first five years are the hardest for any business venture; your venture has about double the usual chance of closing in this time (1 out of 6, rather than 1 out of 12). You will probably have to tighten your belt at home, as well as work long hours and keep careful track of your business expenses. Be careful with your money. Do not take unnecessary risks, play it conservatively, and always keep some capital in reserve for emergencies. The hardest part of a new business, of course, is the learning curve of figuring out what, exactly, you need to do to make a profit, and so the best advice is to have plenty of savings—or a job to provide income—while you learn the ropes.

One thing you should not do is count on venture capitalists or "angel investors," that is, businesspeople who make a living investing on other businesses in the hopes that their equity in the company will increase in value. Venture capitalists have gotten something of a reputation as indiscriminate spendthrifts due to some poor choices made during the dot-com boom of the late 1990s, but the fact is that most do not take risks on unproven products. Rather, they are attracted to young companies that have the potential to become regional or national powerhouses and give better-than-average returns. Nor are venture capitalists are endless sources of money; rather, they are savvy businesspeople who are usually attracted to companies that have already experienced a measure of success. Therefore, it is better to rely on your own resources until you have proven your business will work.

Bookkeeping 101

The principles of double-entry bookkeeping have not changed much since its invention in the fifteenth century: one column records debits, and one records credits. The trick is *doing* it. As a small business owner, you need to be disciplined and meticulous at recording your finances. Thankfully, today there is software available that can do everything from tracking payables and receivables to running checks and generating reports.

Honestly ask yourself if you are the sort of person who does a good job keeping track of finances. If you are not, outsource to a bookkeeping company or hire someone to come in once or twice a week to enter invoices and generate checks for you. Also remember that if you have employees or even freelancers, you will have to file tax forms for them at the end of the year.

Another good idea is to have an accountant for your business to handle advice and taxes (federal, state, local, sales tax, etc.). In fact, consulting with an a certified public accountant is a good idea in general, since they are usually aware of laws and rules that you have never even heard of.

Finally, keep your personal and business accounting separate. If your business ever gets audited, the first thing the IRS looks for is personal expenses disguised as business expenses. A good accountant can help you to know what are legitimate business expenses. Everything you take from the business account, such as payroll and reimbursement, must be recorded and classified.

Being an Employer

Know your situation regarding employees. To begin with, if you have any employees, you will need an Employer Identification Number (EIN), also sometimes called a Federal Tax Identification Number. Getting an EIN is simple: You can fill out IRS form SS-4, or complete the process online at http://www.irs.gov.

Having employees carries other responsibilities and legalities with it. To begin with, you will need to pay payroll taxes (otherwise known as "withholding") to cover income tax, unemployment insurance, Social Security, and Medicare, as well as file W-2 and W-4 forms with the government. You will also be required to pay workman's compensation insurance, and will probably also want to find medical insurance. You are also required to abide by your state's nondiscrimination laws. Most states require you to post nondiscrimination and compensation notices in a public area.

Many employers are tempted to unofficially hire workers "off the books." This can have advantages, but can also mean entering a legal gray area. (Note, however, this is different from hiring freelancers, a temp employed by another company, or having a self-employed professional such as an accountant or bookkeeper come in occasionally to provide a service.) It is one thing to hire the neighbor's teenage son on a one-time basis to help you move some boxes, but quite another to have full-time workers working on a cash-and-carry basis. Regular wages must be noted in the accounts, and gaps may be questioned in the event of an audit. If the workers are injured on the job, you are not covered by workman's comp, and are thus vulnerable to lawsuits. If the workers you hired are not legal residents, you can also be liable for civil and criminal penalties. In general, it is best to keep your employees as above-board as possible.

Building a Business

Good business practices are essential to success. First off, do not overextend yourself. Be honest about what you can do and in what time frame. Secondly, be a responsible business owner. In general, if there is a problem, it is best to explain matters honestly to your clients than to leave them without word and wondering. In the former case, there is at least the possibility of salvaging your reputation and credibility.

Most business is still built by personal contacts and word of mouth. It is for this reason that maintaining your list of contacts is an essential practice. Even if a particular contact may not be useful at a particular moment, a future opportunity may present itself—or you may be able to send someone else to them. Networking, in other words, is as important when you are the boss as when you are looking for a job yourself. As the owner of a company, having a network means getting services on better terms, knowing where to go if you need help with a particular problem, or simply being in the right place at the right time to exploit an opportunity. Join professional organizations, the local Chamber of Commerce, clubs and community organizations, and learn to play golf. And remember—never burn a bridge.

Advertising is another way to build a business. Planning an ad campaign is not as difficult as you might think: You probably already know your media market and business community. The trick is applying it. Again, go with your instincts. If you never look twice at your local weekly, other people probably do not, either. If you are in a high-tourist area, though, local tourists maps might be a good way to leverage your marketing dollar. Ask other people in your area or market who have business similar to your own. Depending on your focus, you might want to consider everything from AM radio or local TV networks, to national trade publications, to hiring a PR firm for an all-out blitz. By thinking about these questions, you can spend your advertising dollars most effectively.

Nor should you underestimate the power of using the Internet to build your business. It is a very powerful tool for small businesses, potentially reaching vast numbers of people for relatively little outlay of money. Launching a Web site has become the modern equivalent of hanging out your shingle. Even if you are primarily a brick-and-mortar business, a Web presence can still be an invaluable tool—your store or offices will show up on Google searches, plus customers can find directions to visit you in person. Furthermore, the Internet offers the small-business owner many useful tools. Print and design services, order fulfillment, credit card processing, and networking—both personal and in terms of linking to other sites—are all available online. Web advertising can be useful, too, either by advertising on specialty sites that appeal to your audience, or by using services such as Google AdWords.

Amateurish print ads, TV commercials, and Web sites do not speak well of your business. Good media should be well-designed, well-edited, and well-put together. It need not, however, be expensive. Shop around and, again, use your network.

Flexibility is also important. "In general, a business must adapt to changing conditions, find new customers and find new products or services that customers need when the demand for their older products or services diminishes," says James Peck, a Long Island, New York, entrepreneur. In other words, if your original plan is not working out, or if demand falls, see if you can parlay your experience, skills, and physical plant into meeting other needs. People are not the only ones who can change their path in life; organizations can, too.

A Final Word

In business, as in other areas of life, the advice of more experienced people is essential. "I think it really takes three businesses until you know what you're doing," Drew Curtis confides. "I sure didn't know what I was doing the first time." Listen to what others have to say, no matter whether it is about your Web site or your business plan. One possible solution is seeking out a mentor, someone who has previously launched a success-ful venture in this field. In any case, before taking any step, ask as many people as many questions as you can. Good advice is invaluable.

Further Resources

American Independent Business Alliance
http://www.amiba.net

American Small Business League
http://www.asbl.com

IRS Small Business and Self-Employed One-Stop Resource
http://www.irs.gov/businesses/small/index.html

The Riley Guide: Steps in Starting Your Own Business
http://www.rileyguide.com/steps.html

Small Business Administration
http://www.sba.gov

Appendix B

Outfitting Yourself for Career Success

As you contemplate a career shift, the first component is to assess your interests. You need to figure out what makes you tick, since there is a far greater chance that you will enjoy and succeed in a career that taps into your passions, inclinations, natural abilities, and training. If you have a general idea of what your interests are, you at least know in which direction you want to travel. You may know you want to simply switch from one sort of nursing to another, or change your life entirely and pursue a dream you have always held. In this case, you can use a specific volume of The Field Guides to Finding a New Career to discover which position to target. If you are unsure of your direction you want to take, well, then the entire scope of the series is open to you! Browse through to see what appeals to you, and see if it matches with your experience and abilities.

The next step you should take is to make a list—do it once in writing—of the skills you have used in a position of responsibility that transfer to the field you are entering. People in charge of interviewing and hiring may well understand that the skills they are looking for in a new hire are used in other fields, but you must spell it out. Most job descriptions are partly a list of skills. Map your experience into that, and very early in your contacts with a prospective employer explicitly address how you acquired your relevant skills. Pick a relatively unimportant aspect of the job to be your ready answer for where you would look forward to learning within the organization, if this seems essentially correct. When you transfer into a field, softly acknowledge a weakness while relating your readiness to learn, but never lose sight of the value you offer both in your abilities and in the freshness of your perspective.

Energy and Experience

The second component in career-switching success is energy. When Jim Fulmer was 61, he found himself forced to close his piano-repair business. However, he was able to parlay his knowledge of music, pianos, and the musical instruments industry into another job as a sales representative for a large piano manufacturer, and quickly built up a clientele of musical-instrument retailers throughout the East Coast. Fulmer's experience highlights another essential lesson for career-changers: There are plenty of opportunities out there, but jobs will not come to you—especially the career-oriented, well-paying ones. You have to seek them out.

Jim Fulmer's case also illustrates another important point: Former training and experience can be a key to success. "Anyone who has to make a career change in any stage of life has to look at what skills they have acquired but may not be aware of," he says. After all, people can more easily change into careers similar to the ones they are leaving. Training and experience also let you enter with a greater level of seniority, provided you have the other necessary qualifications. For instance, a nurse who is already experienced with administering drugs and their benefits and drawbacks, and who is also graced with the personality and charisma to work with the public, can become a pharmaceutical company sales representative.

Unlock Your Network

The next step toward unlocking the perfect job is networking. The term may be overused, but the idea is as old as civilization. More than other animals, humans need one another. With the Internet and telephone, never in history has it been easier to form (or revive) these essential links. One does not have to gird oneself and attend reunion-type events (though for many this is a fine tactic)—but keep open to opportunities to meet people who may be friendly to you in your field. Ben Franklin understood the principal well—*Poor Richard's Almanac* is something of a treatise on the importance or cultivating what Franklin called "friendships" with benefactors. So follow in the steps of the founding fathers and make friends to get ahead. Remember: helping others feels good; it's often the receiving that gets a little tricky. If you know someone particularly well-connected in your field, consider tapping one or two less important connections first so that you make the most of the important one. As you proceed, keep your strengths foremost in your mind because the glue of commerce is mutual interest.

Eighty percent of job openings are *never advertised*, and, according to the U.S. Bureau of Labor statistics, more than half all employees landed their jobs through networking. Using your personal contacts is far more efficient and effective than trusting your résumé to the Web. On the Web, an employer needs to sort through tens of thousands—or millions—of résumés. When you direct your application to one potential employer, you are directing your inquiry to one person who already knows you. The personal touch is everything: Human beings are social animals, programmed to "read" body language; we are naturally inclined to trust those we meet in person, or who our friends and coworkers have recommended. While Web sites can be useful (for looking through help-wanted ads, for instance), expecting employers to pick you out of the slush pile is as effective as throwing your résumé into a black hole.

Do not send your résumé out just to make yourself feel like you're doing something. The proper way to go about things is to employ discipline and order, and then to apply your charm. Begin your networking efforts by making a list of people you can talk to: colleagues, coworkers, and supervisors, people you have had working relationship with, people from church, athletic teams, political organizations, or other community groups, friends, and relatives. You can expand your networking opportunities by following the suggestions in each chapter of the volumes. Your goal here is not so much to land a job as to expand your possibilities and knowledge: Though the people on your list may not be in the position to help you themselves, they might know someone who is. Meeting with them might also help you understand traits that matter and skills that are valued in the field in which you are interested. Even if the person is a potential employer, it is best to phrase your request as if you were seeking information: "You might not be able to help me, but do you know someone I could talk to who could tell me more about what it is like to work in this field?" Being hungry gives one impression, being desperate quite another.

Keep in mind that networking is a two-way street. If you meet someone who had an opening that is not right for you, but if you could recommend someone else, you have just added to your list two people who will be favorably disposed toward you in the future. Also, bear in mind that *you* can help people in *your* old field, thus adding to your own contacts list.

Networking is especially important to the self-employed or those who start their own businesses. Many people in this situation begin because they either recognize a potential market in a field that they are familiar with, or because full-time employment in this industry is no longer a possibility. Already being well-established in a field can help, but so can asking connections for potential work and generally making it known that you are ready, willing, and able to work. Working your professional connections, in many cases, is the *only* way to establish yourself. A freelancer's network, in many cases, is like a spider's web. The spider casts out many strands, since he or she never knows which one might land the next meal.

Dial-Up Help

In general, it is better to call contacts directly than to e-mail them. E-mails are easy for busy people to ignore or overlook, even if they do not mean to. Explain your situation as briefly as possible (see the discussion of the "elevator speech"), and ask if you could meet briefly, either at their office or at a neutral place such as a café. (Be sure that you pay the bill in such a situation—it is a way of showing you appreciate their time and effort.) If you get someone's voicemail, give your "elevator speech" and then say you will call back in a few days to follow up—and then do so. If you reach your contact directly and they are too busy to speak or meet with you, make a definite appointment to call back at a later date. Be persistent, but not annoying.

Once you have arranged a meeting, prep yourself. Look at industry publications both in print and online, as well as news reports (here, GoogleNews, which lets you search through online news reports, can be very handy). Having up-to-date information on industry trends shows that you are dedicated, knowledgeable, and focused. Having specific questions on employers and requests for suggestions will set you apart from the rest of the job-hunting pack. Knowing the score—for instance, asking about the value of one sort of certification instead of another—pegs you as an "insider," rather than a dilettante, someone whose name is worth remembering and passing along to a potential employer.

Finally, set the right mood. Here, a little self-hypnosis goes a long way: Look at yourself in the mirror, and tell yourself that you are an enthusiastic, committed professional. Mood affects confidence and performance. Discipline your mind so you keep your perspective and self-respect. Nobody wants to hire someone who comes across as insincere, tells a sob story, or is still in the doldrums of having lost their previous

job. At the end of any networking meeting, ask for someone else who might be able to help you in your journey to finding a position in this field, either with information or a potential job opening.

Get a Lift

When you meet with a contact in person (as well as when you run into anyone by chance who may be able to help you), you need an "elevator speech" (so-named because it should be short enough to be delivered during an elevator ride from a ground level to a high floor). This is a summary in which, in less than two minutes, you give them a clear impression of who you are, where you come from, your experience and goals, and why you are on the path you are on. The motto above Plato's Academy holds true: Know Thyself (this is where our Career Compasses and guides will help you). A long and rambling "elevator story" will get you nowhere. Furthermore, be positive: Neither a sad-sack story nor a tirade explaining how everything that went wrong in your old job is someone else's fault will get you anywhere. However, an honest explanation of a less-than-fortunate circumstance, such as a decline in business forcing an office closing, needing to change residence to a place where you are not qualified to work in order to further your spouse's career, or needing to work fewer hours in order to care for an ailing family member, is only honest.

An elevator speech should show 1) you know the business involved; 2) you know the company; 3) you are qualified (here, try to relate your education and work experience to the new situation); and 4) you are goal-oriented, dependable, and hardworking. Striking a balance is important; you want to sound eager, but not overeager. You also want to show a steady work experience, but not that you have been so narrowly focused that you cannot adjust. Most important is emphasizing what you can do for the company. You will be surprised how much information you can include in two minutes. Practice this speech in front of a mirror until you have the key points down perfectly. It should sound natural, and you should come across as friendly, confident, and assertive. Finally, remember eye contact! Good eye contact needs to be part of your presentation, as well as your everyday approach when meeting potential employers and leads.

Get Your Résumé Ready

Everyone knows what a résumé is, but how many of us have really thought about how to put one together? Perhaps no single part of the job search is subject to more anxiety—or myths and misunderstandings—than this 8 ½-by-11-inch sheet of paper.

On the one hand, it is perfectly all right for someone—especially in certain careers, such as academia—to have a résumé that is more than one page. On the other hand, you do not need to tell a future employer *everything*. Trim things down to the most relevant; for a 40-year-old to mention an internship from two decades ago is superfluous. Likewise, do not include irrelevant jobs, lest you seem like a professional career-changer.

Tailor your descriptions of your former employment to the particular position you are seeking. This is not to say you should lie, but do make your experience more appealing. If the job you're looking for involves supervising other people, say if you have done this in the past; if it involves specific knowledge or capabilities, mention that you possess these qualities. In general, try to make your past experience seem as similar to what you are seeking.

The standard advice is to put your Job Objective at the heading of the résumé. An alternative to this is a Professional Summary, which some recruiters and employers prefer. The difference is that a Job Objective mentions the position you are seeking, whereas a Professional Summary mentions your background (e.g. "Objective: To find a position as a sales representative in agribusiness machinery" versus "Experienced sales representative; strengths include background in agribusiness, as well as building team dynamics and market expansion"). Of course, it is easy to come up with two or three versions of the same document for different audiences.

The body of the résumé of an experienced worker varies a lot more than it does at the beginning of your career. You need not put your education or your job experience first; rather, your résumé should emphasize your strengths. If you have a master's degree in a related field, that might want to go before your unrelated job experience. Conversely, if too much education will harm you, you might want to bury that under the section on professional presentations you have given that show how good you are at communicating. If you are currently enrolled in a course or other professional development, be sure to note this (as well as your date of expected graduation). A résumé is a study of blurs, highlights, and jewels. You blur everything you must in order to fit the description of your experience to the job posting. You highlight what is relevant from each and any of your positions worth mentioning. The jewels are the little headers and such—craft them, since they are what is seen first.

You may also want to include professional organizations, work-related achievements, and special abilities, such as your fluency in a foreign language. Also mention your computer software qualifications and capabilities, especially if you are looking for work in a technological field or if you are an older job-seeker who might be perceived as behind the technology curve. Including your interests or family information might or might not be a good idea—no one really cares about your bridge club, and in fact they might worry that your marathon training might take away from your work commitments, but, on the other hand, mentioning your golf handicap or three children might be a good idea if your potential employer is an avid golfer or is a family woman herself.

You can either include your references or simply note, "References available upon request." However, be sure to ask your references' permission to use their names and alert them to the fact that they may be contacted before you include them on your résumé! Be sure to include name, organization, phone number, and e-mail address for each contact.

Today, word processors make it easy to format your résumé. However, beware of prepackaged résumé "wizards"—they do not make you stand out in the crowd. Feel free to strike out on your own, but remember the most important thing in formatting a résumé is consistency. Unless you have a background in typography, do not get too fancy. Finally, be sure to have someone (or several people!) read your résumé over for you.

For more information on résumé writing, check out Web sites such as http://www.resume.monster.com.

Craft Your Cover Letter

It is appropriate to include a cover letter with your résumé. A cover letter lets you convey extra information about yourself that does not fit or is not always appropriate in your résumé, such as why you are no longer working in your original field of employment. You can and should also mention the name of anyone who referred you to the job. You can go into some detail about the reason you are a great match, given the job description. Also address any questions that might be raised in the potential employer's mind (for instance, a gap in employment). Do not, however, ramble on. Your cover letter should stay focused on your goal: To offer a strong, positive impression of yourself and persuade the hiring manager that you are worth an interview. Your cover letter gives you a chance to stand out from the other applicants and sell yourself. In fact, according to a CareerBuilder.com survey, 23 percent of hiring managers say a candidate's ability to relate his or her experience to the job at hand is a top hiring consideration.

Even if you are not a great writer, you can still craft a positive yet concise cover letter in three paragraphs: An introduction containing the specifics of the job you are applying for; a summary of why you are a good fit for the position and what you can do for the company; and a closing with a request for an interview, contact information, and thanks. Remember to vary the structure and tone of your cover letter—do not begin every sentence with "I."

Ace Your Interview

In truth, your interview begins well before you arrive. Be sure to have read up well on the company and its industry. Use Web sites and magazines—http://www.hoovers.com offers free basic business information, and trade magazines deliver both information and a feel for the industries they cover. Also, do not neglect talking to people in your circle who might know about trends in the field. Leave enough time to digest the information so that you can give some independent thought to the company's history and prospects. You don't need to expert when you arrive to be interviewed; but you should be comfortable. The most important element of all is to be poised and relaxed during the interview itself. Preparation and practice can help a lot.

Be sure to develop well-thought-through answers to the following, typical interview openers and standard questsions.

☞ Tell me about yourself. (Do not complain about how unsatisfied you were in your former career, but give a brief summary of your applicable background and interest in the particular job area.) If there is a basis to it, emphasize how much you love to work and how you are a team player.

☞ Why do you want this job? (Speak from the brain, and the heart—of course you want the money, but say a little here about what you find interesting about the field and the company's role in it.)

☞ What makes you a good hire? (Remember here to connect the company's needs and your skill set. Ultimately, your selling points probably come down to one thing: you will make your employer money. You want the prospective hirer to see that your skills are valuable not to the world in general but to this specific company's bottom line. What can you do for them?)

☞ What led you to leave your last job? (If you were fired, still try say something positive, such as, "The business went through a challenging time, and some of the junior marketing people were let go.")

Practice answering these and other questions, and try to be genuinely positive about yourself, and patient with the process. Be secure but not cocky; don't be shy about forcing the focus now and then on positive contributions you have made in your working life—just be specific. As with the elevator speech, practice in front of the mirror.

A couple pleasantries are as natural a way as any to start the actual interview, but observe the interviewer closely for any cues to fall silent and formally begin. Answer directly; when in doubt, finish your phrase and look to the interviewer. Without taking command, you can always ask, "Is there more you would like to know?" Your attentiveness will convey respect. Let your personality show too—a positive attitude and a grounded sense of your abilities will go a long way to getting you considered. During the interview, keep your cell phone off and do not look at your watch. Toward the end of your meeting, you may be asked whether you have any questions. It is a good idea to have one or two in mind. A few examples follow:

☞ "What makes your company special in the field?"

☞ "What do you consider the hardest part of this position?"

☞ "Where are your greatest opportunities for growth?"

☞ "Do you know when you might need anything further from me?"

Leave discussion of terms for future conversations. Make a cordial, smooth exit.

Remember to Follow Up

Send a thank-you note. Employers surveyed by CareerBuilder.com in 2005 said it matters. About 15 percent said they would not hire someone who did not follow up with a thanks. And almost 33 percent would think less of a candidate. The form of the note does not much matter—if you know a manager's preference, use it. Otherwise, just be sure to follow up.

Winning an Offer

A job offer can feel like the culmination of a long and difficult struggle. So naturally, when you hear them, you may be tempted to jump at the offer. Don't. Once an employer wants you, he or she will usually give you a chance to consider the offer. This is the time to discuss terms of employment, such as vacation, overtime, and benefits. A little effort now can be well worth it in the future. Be sure to do a check of prevailing salaries for your field and area before signing on. Web sites for this include Payscale.com, Salary.com, and Salaryexpert.com. If you are thinking about asking for better or different terms from what the prospective employer offered, rest assured—that's how business gets done; and it may just burnish the positive impression you have already made.

Index